# ENGAGING YOUTH OF TODAY:
# *MIND CLEAR, BODY FIT, SPIRIT WELL*

## (DESIGNED FOR PARENTS AND PROFESSIONALS)

## Dr. James Sapp

Illustrations by:
Scott Martindale
Designsfrompine.com

ISBN 978-1-64559-044-6 (Paperback)
ISBN 978-1-64559-045-3 (Digital)



Covenant Books, Inc.
11661 Hwy 707
Murrells Inlet, SC 29576
www.covenantbooks.com

# Contents

# PREFACE

At times, it is difficult to engage and connect with children and adolescents whether this is your own or someone else's. Therefore, youth pastors, laypersons, social workers, counselors, psychologists, teachers, and anyone who is in the helping profession or who simply cares about engaging or connecting with children and adolescents (hereafter referred to as *youth*) could benefit by memorizing some simple engaging communication techniques that have worked for me during my thirty years of experience in working with youth. These techniques are easy ways to memorize and recall what to say to *youth* in a nonthreatening, nonjudgmental manner while maintaining a caring and empathic attitude.

When engaging youth, it is important to remember that your body language is communicating and is actually speaking louder than your words are for the complex youth of today. Furthermore, it is imperative not to overreact but to act simply when trying to engage youth. If a person really cares about and wants to know the youth of today, the caring person must sincerely listen and hear the message being sent by the youth.

Although the ideas presented in this book are not a panacea, I believe that since they have worked for me, when engaging to students, foster children, clients, and patients, as well as other youth on a day to day basis, I hope the ideas presented will work for you and the youth you encounter in your life, irrelevant of the environment or setting. Additionally, please remember that you must be sincere in using these ideas to the youth who will know that you are not genuine which will not afford the opportunity to engage the youth. By not being truthful, you will most likely not be trusted by the youth. More importantly, you will reinforce the belief that youth of today have in their subculture which is that all adults are hypocrites and not worthy of trust; thus, honesty is the best policy when attempting to engage youth of today.

I hope you enjoy memorizing and practicing the ideas presented in this book as you work with youth to better their lives. It is fun to practice using role plays and role reversals with your adult friends, significant others, or your coworkers. As you are in a role play, be sure to get feedback from other adults that will focus mainly on what you did well and how you might improve your style.

We are our worst self-critic, so be sure to pick a practice partner who will focus on what you did well! It is even beneficial to practice these techniques alone in front of a mirror, so you can see how your body language is or is not in sync with the words exiting your mouth. Feel free to videotape or record yourself to see how you are doing. But again, be sure to focus on the positives in your self-recorded practices. Finally, if you have any feedback, for me, after you read and practice mastering these new skills, I welcome what worked for you as well as additional ideas you have, especially since we all have the common goal of engaging the disengaged youth as we all continue to learn in this ever-changing world of postmodern development.

When approaching youth of today, three keys must be followed and adhered to: first, your mind should be clear. There should be no distractions; second, your body should be fit. There should be no hunger, pains, or other physical distractions that draws the attention to you, rather than maintaining the focus on the youth; and finally, your spirit should be well. You need to have good intentions when engaging youth. Your spirit needs to be in the right place, not deceiving or being vindictive. Your love will show the youth that your spirit is well.

So with a *clear mind*, *fit body*, and *well-spirited* approach to youth, you can now engage them whether you are a parent, professional, or both. Be positive! This means *Mind Clear. Body Fit. Spirit Well.* When you are positive in all three areas, then and only then, you will be able to tell your story of how you were able to engage and connect with the disengaged youth of today!

# Understanding Youth Through a Developmental Lens—A Quick Overview

When working with youth, it is important to remember to view them from a holistic perspective, which includes psychosocial, cognitive, psychosexual, moral, and spiritual or faith stages of development.

An in-depth and detailed discussion of these areas of development are far beyond the scope of this book. However, the basics of the developmental theories will be covered in order to support you as you engage the youth of today while assisting them in their healing and growth. First, we will briefly look at the developmental theories of Erikson's psychosocial stages, followed by Piaget's cognitive, Freud's psychosexual, Kohlberg's moral, and Fowler's faith developmental stage theories. We will then conclude with Bronfenbrenner's bioecological systems perspective because his theory is also important in assisting adults with understanding the contextual scenario in which the youth, they are working with resides. It is important to note, however, that although most of these are stage models of development, each youth is different and unique from the other even if they are chronologically the same age; they may be on a different level of development cognitively, socially, or spiritually.

Therefore, just because a youth may be fourteen years of age does not mean that he or she fits into the age bracket within each table described for each developmental theory. In addition, be sure to approach each youth on their developmental level because talking over or under their age bracket may insult them or they may simply not understand which may shut them down that the opportunity they engage will be missed. Thus, the disengaged youth will remain disengaged from you, the adult who they need to connect to in order to grow in a positive direction.

# DEVELOPMENTAL THEORIES

Erik Erikson—Psychosocial Developmental Stages

This is a *psychosocial* approach to development that was one of the first developmental theories that covered the whole lifespan.

In table 1, you will find a chart that covers ages birth through adolescence. I have included all earlier stages here because Erikson believed that if earlier crises were not resolved, then the person would have more difficulty with the other stages of development.

I would agree with his conclusion on this matter since I have seen it over the years in working with youth as well as adults. So it is important for you to see what stage the youth may be stuck in or needing to work through in order to know how to approach the youth for engaging him or her and assisting them in getting back on track to a healthy trajectory.

Table 1

| Stage Name | Age Range | Notes |
|---|---|---|
| Trust vs. Mistrust | Birth–18 months | This is the oral-sensory mode. Hope that basic needs are met (e.g., feeding and affection) is the basic strength of this stage and develops trust. |
| Autonomy vs. Shame | 18 months–3 years | This is the anal-urethra mode. Will is the basic strength of this stage. (e.g., Developing a sense of control leads to autonomy while failure to begin to be independent leads to shame and doubt.) |
| Initiative vs. Guilt | 3–7 years | The playing age. Purpose is the basic strength of this stage. (e.g., Exerting control over their environment leads to a sense of purpose. Too much power results in disapproval leading to guilt.) |

| Industry vs. Inferiority | 7–10 years | The school age. Competence is the basic strength of this stage. (e.g., This is achieved when they do well in meeting academic and social demands.) |
|---|---|---|
| Identity vs. Identity Confusion | Adolescence | Finding out "Who I am?" and staying true to the self is the basic strength of this stage. |

I think it is important to include a brief example of a youth that is dealing with a crisis at each stage to assist you in being able to apply this theory.

For the trust versus mistrust then, an example might look like an infant who is crying because she is hungry, and her diaper needs changed. The caregiver who leaves this female infant and does not tend to the hunger or diaper change needs results in the infant not trusting her world that her needs will not be met. She, therefore, learns to distrust her world which carries into later stages of life.

For autonomy versus shame and doubt, an example might be a two-year-old boy attempts to go use the toilet alone and the parent does not permit this to occur. Therefore, the toddler learns shame and cannot develop a sense of independence. Later in life, this may result in the boy developing into a dependent person because he doubts himself and his abilities.

For the initiative versus guilt stage, the child must be able to explore their environment. A crisis may be developed when the child exerts too much power and is quickly shut down by the caregiver resulting in the child feeling guilty. If this continues and poor parenting skills play a role, then the child may continue to feel guilty in other stages of development since he has not worked through this specific crisis. Appropriate boundaries need to be established to assist this child in working through the psychosocial crisis.

During the industry versus inferiority stage or the school-aged children, they must work with others and learn to cope with academic and social demands. Failure to do so appropriately may result in a sense of negative self and inferiority as the youth compare their talents and abilities to others. The youth who fails at a task playing a sport or doing a science project, compares themselves to others, and realizes that he is not that good resulting in feelings of inferiority. This, in turn, can lead to low self-esteem and even depression or anxiety. If the youth is always praised even when they fail, they may develop an unhealthy personality, such as narcissism, which in turn, can lead to aggression and bullying.

Finally, the stage of identity versus identity confusion is quite complex, and anyone that has gone through puberty and adolescence knows how difficult becoming who you want or need to be is.

We have all tried on different identities to some degrees. Some go to the extreme and against the family value of religion dressing in gothic clothes or obtaining piercings when the family rule does not permit such values. Others try a different personality, and the parents may shut this new persona down demanding that the youth does not explore who he or she wants to be, but rather the youth is told that everyone in this family is pleasant and a helper so you too shall be in the helping profession of. For instance, nursing or teaching children with disabilities. Thus, the youth is not given permission to explore different selves and to become who they truly might want to be. Failure to be able to become their true self may result in a weak youth or a weak sense of self as well as a youth who is confused about their role.

When working with adolescents, more than likely, they are in this stage of development where they are forming their identity, and as such, it is important to not only let them explore their selves but also to not overreact if his nails are black and her hair is multicolored lest you push them further away from you with minimal hope of connecting to them.

## Jean Piaget—Cognitive Stages of Development

This is a *cognitive* approach to development that covers the lifespan.

Below in table 2, you will find information that covers ages birth through adolescence. Earlier stages are included because a youth may be diagnosed with an intellectual developmental disorder or an intellectual disorder (formerly mental retardation or MR) or may have a learning disability.

By understanding these issues, the youth suffers from what you can see at which stage you need to approach to the youth. If there are no developmental delays, impairments, or issues, then the adult may proceed engaging the youth at their level of cognitive functioning.

Piaget's theory includes substages at each of the four main stages, but they are not covered here due to the complexity of his model, which is as previously mentioned, beyond the scope of this book. I refer you to read any lifespan development or developmental psychology textbook for a dccpcr discussion and overview of Piaget's substages.

Table 2

| Stage Name | Age Range | Notes |
| --- | --- | --- |
| Sensorimotor | Birth–2 years | Infants learn to coordinate their senses and their motor behavior. |
| Preoperational | 2–7 years | The child gains the ability to use symbolic representations for objects and events that are not physically present. |
| Operational | 7–12 years | The child represents objects mentally and engage in logical reasoning about the world around them through the use of these mental representations, but they are not yet able to think abstractly. |
| Formal Operational | Adolescence–Adulthood | Abstract thinking occurs for most but not all. |

What is important to note about the formal operational stage is that not all adolescents will achieve it; likewise, not even all adults are abstract thinkers all the time. Sometimes we are cognizant misers and want a simple concrete explanation so we do not have to think as much; we want to reserve our cognitive abilities in case we need to rely on them at a later date. Likewise, it is plausible that the youth is also reserving their cognitive *brain cells* for other daily issues that they enjoy, like chatting with friends or taking selfies. I mean, after all, it does take a lot of preparation to get that selfie just right to impress others!

Also, thinking too much does give some people headaches and makes them irritable so there seems to be some justification for all of us being a little misery when it comes to our cognitive abilities. Therefore, approaching youth at the concrete operational stage may be the best at times.

You can always adjust to preoperational or abstract stage of cognition as appropriate to the specific needs of the youth, such as a sufferer of autism spectrum disorder, intellectual developmental disability, or on the other end of the continuum, even a gifted child. Ask for a verbal acknowledgment from the youth to ensure you are using the correct cognitive level of approach.

## Sigmund Freud—Psychosexual Stages of Development

This is a *psychosexual* approach to development that spreads throughout the lifespan.

In table 3 below, you will find information that covers ages birth through adolescence. You may note that Freud's psychosexual stages of development stopped at the genital stage, which applies to those who reached puberty and beyond it.

It is of note that this theory was developed during the Victorian era, and that some not only do not approve of this theory but also even believe that there is no validity in it. Some would even argue that Freud's theory of development should not be taught. However, I have included it here because I will leave it to your own judgment about whether or not this may apply to the youth you are working with. I find it useful because, for instance, a youth may be orally or anally fixated. Thus, I can investigate and see from the youth's history if any cause of the fixation can be found.

An example of oral fixation can be a youth who chews on pens and pencils until they are destroyed or who must smoke cigarettes or "cigarillos."

Anal fixation at the extreme may be when a youth is too clean and suffers from obsessive compulsive disorder or OCD. At the other extreme of anal fixation is a youth who is very messy to the point of nastiness and disorder everywhere. Either way, the adult needs to keep this in mind when engaging the youth in order to get at what may have happened at an earlier stage of development that may have caused this issue to arise.

Given these examples, therefore, I do see some merits in Freud's psychosexual stage theory of development. Having a clear mind, fit body, and well spirit while working through the youth's fixation without judgment is important in order to engage the youth.

The fixations can be difficult for the youth to discuss, so it is best to maintain your laid-back self during these talks.

Table 3

| Stage Name | Age Range | Notes |
|---|---|---|
| Oral | 0–18 months | Oral-sensory, both receiving and accepting. (e.g., Conflict and fixation can arise when the oral needs of the youth are not met.) |
| Anal | 18 months–3 years | Behave both impulsively and compulsively. (e.g., Toilet training is important, and the youth can become anally expulsive or anally retentive (OCD) during this stage.) |

| Phallic | 3–6 years | Play age with an interest in the genital area and more freedom in their ability to move around. (e.g., Stimulation of their own genitals and attraction toward their opposite sex.) |
|---|---|---|
| Latency | 6 years–Puberty | Sexual development is latent during the school age. Children use their energies to learn about their culture and education is the focus. (e.g., Youth get pleasure from their social interactions with their peers and repress interests in sexuality. This may not be true for those who have been sexually abused. Sexual acting out may occur.) |
| Genital | Puberty–Adulthood | Genital maturation occurs. (e.g., Sexual exploration with others outside of the family.) |

## Lawrence Kohlberg—Moral Developmental Stages

This is a *moral* approach to development that covers the lifespan.

Though in table 4, you will find information that only covers ages five through adolescence.

Kohlberg's detailed theory includes three levels, each of which had a couple of substages embedded in them.

The three main levels are only covered here because, again, the complexity of the theory is beyond the scope of this book. However, you may review Kohlberg's full theory in most developmental psychology or lifespan development textbooks. I believe it is an interesting read, and he offers some good examples as to how he concluded at what level of morality each youth was functioning under.

Table 4

| Stage Name | Age Range | Notes |
|---|---|---|
| Preconventional level | Childhood | Adherence to standards to avoid punishment or receive reinforcement. |
| Conventional level | Adolescence | Internalization of standards and values gain approval or avoid disapproval duty to society. |

| Postconventional level | Usually adulthood | Complete internalization of control over moral conduct affirms agreed upon rights and finally affirms own ethical principles. (Many do not achieve these levels.) |
|---|---|---|

Let me explain a little about what to ask the youth to see which level he or she may be functioning in.

The Heinz dilemma was used by Kohlberg and is a good example to go through the main stages to get a sense of the youth's moral developmental stage.

The gist of the story is that an elderly man's wife was dying. The pharmacist had the cure, but it cost too much for the elderly man to purchase. The pharmacist said he was going to make money from this drug. Heinz tried to borrow the money but could not raise the two thousand dollars. So he broke into the pharmacist's lab and stole the drug for his wife who was dying.

After telling the story, you ask the youth, "Should Heinz have broken into the pharmacist's lab and stolen the drug for his wife? Why or why not?"

It is not important for the responder to answer what Heinz should *do*, but rather the *justification* the responder offers are what is important and will reveal at what stage the youth is functioning.

As an example of a Heinz dilemma response from the preconventional level then is when a youth answers the Heinz question with the response in favor of stealing: "If you let your wife die, you will get in trouble" (avoiding punishment) or against Heinz's stealing: "You'll get caught for stealing and go to jail."

An example from the conventional level might be when a youth in favor of stealing replies, "You won't let your wife die because you are afraid to do what will save her. It's about honor," or a youth against Heinz's stealing at this level might state, "You'll feel guilty for breaking the law and being dishonest."

## James Fowler—Faith Stages of Development

This is a *faith* approach to development that covers the entire lifespan.

In table 5, you will find information that only covers ages two through adolescence though. This is a very in-depth theory and will not be covered in detail here. I would refer you to my dissertation or to some writings by Fowler himself, although there are some developmental textbooks out there that have begun to include Fowler's theory in them. You just have to search for it on the web.

Now although some adults do not see a need to review faith beliefs with youth, I think it is very valuable; however, it is important to be open-minded with youth about their belief system because what I have found in my research is that there is something innate in us that leads us to ask big questions throughout the lifespan as we search for purpose and meaning in life.

Therefore, I recommend knowing the basics and allowing youth to share their thoughts about spirit and faith while keeping an open mind in order to engage the youth in civil discussion.

Of course, some agencies do not allow for discussion of religion with a youth unless parental or guardian permission is granted, so be sure to check with the agency you work for. If you do not work for an agency or are not a professional, you still need to be cautious when discussing religion or faith with youth.

We live in such a litigious society it is a shame that this can hinder healthy dialogue and engagement of youth. So just be careful and again, be open minded when discussing this important part of development.

Table 5

| Stage Name | Age Range | Notes |
| --- | --- | --- |
| Intuitive-Projective Faith | 2–7 years | At this stage, children identify with characters and fragments of stories but can neither create, retell stories in a linear fashion, nor identify the main point of a story. |
| Mythic-Literal Faith | 7–12 years | Reasoning is concrete and literal. |
| Synthetic-Conventional Faith | Adolescence | The adolescent can articulate metanarratives (e.g., understanding that the Bible is one story rather than a collection of many stories) and distinguish different systems of values. |

## Urie Bronfenbrenner—Bioecological Systems Perspective

This is a *bioecological systems* approach to development that affects each of us, youth and adults.

Below, you will find figure 1 that explains the context in which youth develop in order to assist you in understanding how relationships are *bidirectional* and what areas of their life may be negative and what may be strengths. In other words, there are many systems impacting the youth's development. In addition, it is not only what the youth does or says that influences the adult, but it is also what the adult says or the way in which the adult acts that has an impact, whether positive or negative, on the youth. Thus, interactions are *bidirectional*, going both ways between a youth and an adult as indicated with arrows in figure 1.

Put in another way, to-and-from and from-and-to simultaneously—in this bioecological systems perspective, the individual or *youth* is in the center. What is important here, for instance, is the youth's age, gender, and health.

Then the next system is called the *microsystem*. This is where the school the youth attends as well as peers, church group, and health services are in play. The *mesosystem* is the interaction of these systems. The next layer in the figure is the *exosystem* which is where the extended family, mass media, guardians' work environment, neighborhood, and friends of the family would fit. The last system is called the *macrosystem* and is the economics, culture, history, and laws of the land that are having an impact or not on the youth. The *chronosystem* is not a system, but it is the time since life events that have had an impact or are currently having an impact on the youth. Examples are life transitions (divorce of parents, puberty, and even going from junior or middle school to high school), as well as historical events.

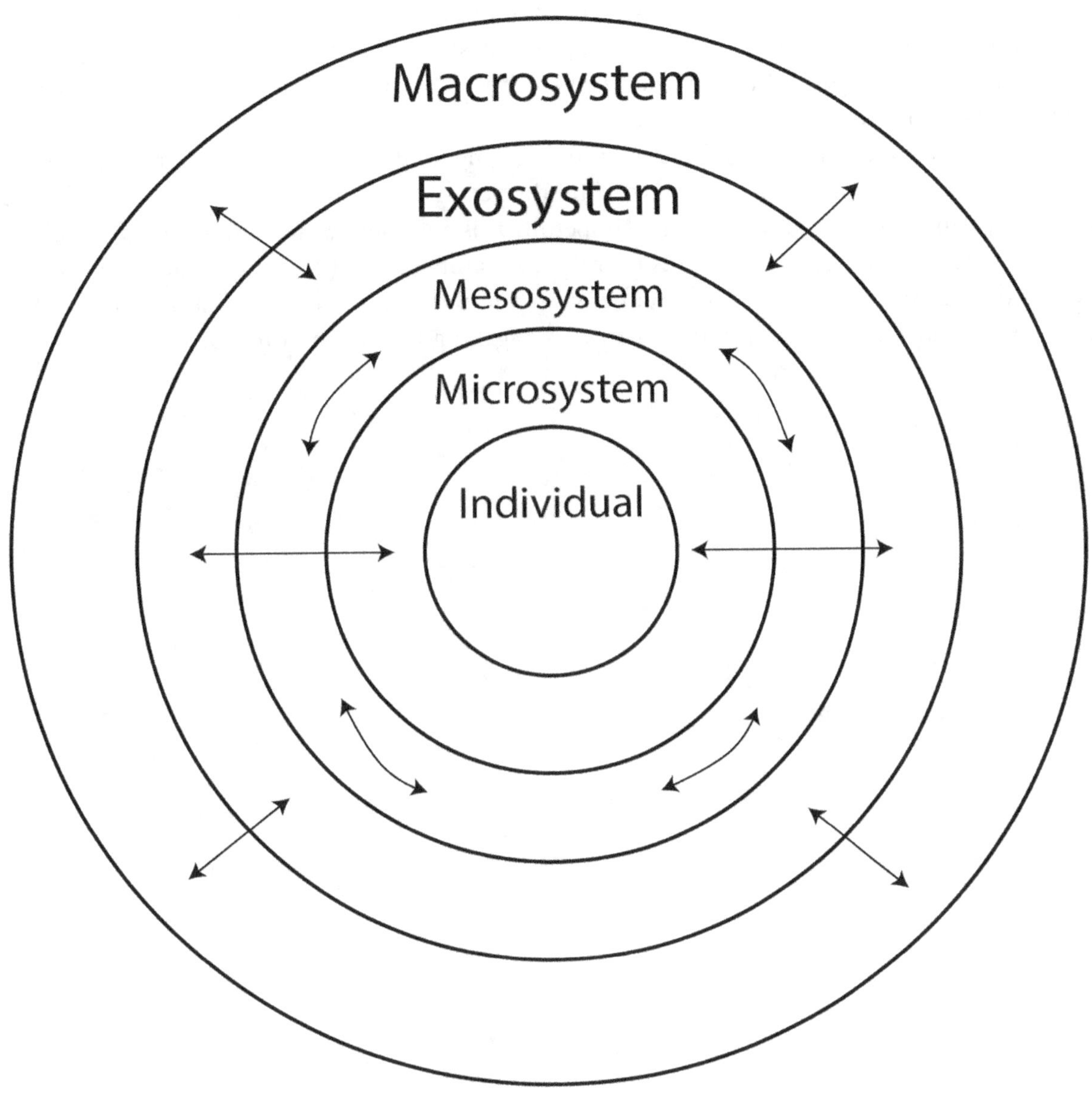



# BRONFENBRENNER

Now that you have reviewed a basic understanding of developmental theories, be sure to review them often so you can memorize them if you desire to engage youth effectively and at appropriate levels of development. Remember, it is very important to look through the correct developmental lens in order to understand the youth you are trying to engage and connect with lest your interaction be a blur. The idea is to keep it simple by having a clear mind, fit body, and well spirit while being sure to focus on the youth and their specific developmental level.

The next section of this book will assist you in engaging youth and maintaining that connection once established. In turn, the connection between you and the youth can be grown and strengthened as your relationship develops and becomes healthier. Thus, hopefully this will then form a long-term and lasting positive relationship that the youth desires and needs in order to maintain his or her engagement with other adults. As a result of this engagement and connection between you the adult and the youth, the youth can become a productive member of society and, in turn, work on engaging the youth of tomorrow.

# WHEN ENGAGING YOUTH AND MAINTAINING THEIR ENGAGEMENT

## When Engaging a Youth, Try a Little TLC but more PCT.

You have probably heard the expression "show them a little TLC" or "show some tender, love, and care" somewhere before in your life. Likewise, you have possibly heard people say that this is how we should treat others with love.

Well, keeping it real in your discussions between you and the youth by being sincere and genuine is like using TLC. But adults need to take it even further by adding a little PCT.

Carl Rogers, who developed Rogerian or person-centered therapy (PCT), gave us some important concepts to use when working with disengaged people in the helping profession. But any adult, not simply professionals, can implement these concepts when attempting to engage youth. Rogers developed PCT on the idea that for relationships, especially therapeutic ones to flourish, one must be genuine, authentic, and be willing to accept another unconditionally while at the same time displaying empathy. Thus, these concepts of PCT must be applied to the ever so cautious youth of today if a person is ever going to make progress in connecting to any part of the youth's life. In fact, research has shown us professionals in the helping field that it is not so much about technique in therapy as much as it is about relationship building and maintenance through the PCT approach.

What are the better ways to build a relationship with youth by being authentic and honest? Isn't it nice to know that someone would accept you unconditionally? More importantly, have not the youth of today been judged enough by their own peers? You can have means of connecting to and thus assisting the hurting youth if you show them unconditional acceptance. They will open up to you like you have never seen before when you accept them as they are in the moment. I have seen this in my experience time and time again! This unconditional acceptance allows you both to connect.

One way to get the youth to disclose to you is to act interested in them by asking open-ended questions and by reframing or paraphrasing what was just stated by the youth. For instance, you will get much more information from asking an open question rather than a closed question such as "What is your favorite color?" The response will be their favorite color. That's it. Nothing else to add because it is a closed question! But if you ask an open-ended question such as "Tell me what your favorite color is and tell me about your color." This will get you more information from the youth than a closed question.

Another example of a closed question is "How was your day?" with a response of "Fine." Ending the conversation, even though we know that their day was more than likely not fine at all. The open question would be best here such as, "Tell me about your day at school. What did you do exactly and what was it like for you?" Can you see how the latter of the two will likely get you more information and conversation than a closed question? You can always add a phrase like "Tell me more about that if you would please?" The message you are sending the youth is that you are interested in what they have to say and more importantly that you want to be a part of their life because you are interested in them as a human being.

At times, you may hear some words that you do not approve of and you can deal with this appropriately by using what we call gentle confrontation. This will allow the avenues of communication to remain open if you do not overreact and begin to judge them. Remember, the goal is to get them to talk to you, so do not shut them down as this may be the only opportunity you have to engage them.

Gentle confrontation needs to be used only when necessary. You can still maintain the relationship developed when gentle confrontation is used appropriately. The adult should display a calm voice and moderate eye contact. Never use physical restraint unless there is a safety issue, risk of harm to self or others, and only if approved and granted permission by proper authorities or administration of an agency. At times, instead of gentle confrontation, the adult can choose to actively ignore a comment made by the youth. The youth may be looking for a shock reaction, so it is time to keep your poker face on as the expression goes. This requires that you do not show any emotion nor flinch. If you do this, the youth will read you and just like in the game of poker, once read, you lost the hand and maybe even the game. Remember, you can always address the inappropriate comment later.

My experience in working with youth tells me that when I ignore and do not make an issue of the comment, it tends to increase the trust level and move closer to engaging the youth. At other times, I have ignored inappropriate comments and found the youth to apologize and not make inappropriate statements in my presence in the future. This would, of course, maintain the engagement we have with the youth and this is what we want to accomplish.

Also, appropriate humor is important when engaging youth. They can be quite sensitive in the teen years, so be careful how you use humor when interacting with youth. If you pick on their looks, like hairstyle or clothes, you may risk losing the opportunity to engage and connect with the youth. Yes, at times, this does work out fine but be sure you know enough about the youth before you make a comment that might offend their fragile egos. Remember, they are developing and teens are trying out their identities. (See previous tables on Freud and Erikson.)

## When Maintaining the Youth's Engagement

First, remember *their* story. That's right! This is about them and *their story*, not you or your story when trying to maintain connections made. Recall as much as you can about the youth that you are talking to, and if you forgot a part of their story, then ask them to tell it to you again at an appropriate time and place. Remember, you do not want to embarrass the youth because they will remember this and may even use it against you later when they share with other youth their thoughts about you, the adult. This may then cause you to not be able to engage with other youth because you have lost your credibility based on what another youth said about you. If this happens, it will be difficult to earn the youth's trust and this then will result in a long struggle to attempt to engage the difficult youth.

A second means to maintain engagement with youth is to use a type of behavior modification, such as positive reinforcement and what we professionals call "catching them being good."

Behavior modification should be used when the youth is changing their attitude or behavior. Adults need to use positive reinforcement, such as giving praise when you catch them being good and not misbehaving. Youth have received attention but so much of it has been negative attention. And when you attempt to approach them in a positive frame of mind, they may be suspicious and not open up to you. However, they will start to realize that it is *attention* you are giving them and may like the *positive* approach rather than all the negative attention they received. Either way, be sure to start focusing on catching them being good and ignoring negative seeking behaviors if there is not a safety issue involved.

Youth want and seek attention from adults and even older youth. In their minds, negative attention is better than none at all! If this is true, then why not focus more on the positive and see some good results come to fruition?

One of the best ways I have found to connect with youth is to empathize with them. To empathize is to feel what they are feeling. This may be difficult for some adults to do.

The best way to do this is to listen to the youth explaining what they are feeling and then putting yourself in their shoes.

There are several opportunities for this, like the following examples:

- What would it feel like to be bullied?
- What would it be like to grow up in a home where their parents argue all the time?
- What would it be like to not be able to trust an adult because the youth has been physically abused?
- What would it be like to not be able to trust an adult because the youth has been sexually abused by an authority figure?
- What would it be like to not fit in with peers at school because the youth feels different?

The adult needs to use the same eye lenses of the youth's glasses to see what it would be like to have experienced their pain and empathize, not sympathize. It is important to note that PCT is not only good to begin engaging but also for maintaining the engagement and connection made between you and the youth. A little PCT goes a long way in working with youth, so be sure to share it with them.

# HALT AND SOLER

In graduate school numerous years ago, I heard about an acronym called *HALT* and believed that this applies to adults who desire to engage youth. An adult will need to ensure that she or he is *not HALT*. This means that you, as the adult, need to make sure you are *not* **H**ungry, **A**ngry, **L**onely, or **T**ired when you want to engage youth.

There are several reasons why *HALT* is dangerous not only when being around youth, but especially when attempting to engage this population. If any of these issues exist, it is best to not engage the youth. Reasons to hold off attempting to engage youth at a specific time is when you are distracted not listening, empathizing, and being genuine or real, maybe you are even apathetic. All these issues lead to the youth sensing that you really do not care and may make them question why you are even attempting to engage in his or her world.

To avoid *HALT*, be sure to engage in self-care: eat appropriate healthy meals and snacks, address your own anger and leave it outside the discussion while engaging the youth, and remember to not get your needs met when working with youth as this may range from being unethical to immoral. Your personal loneliness is not their issue; and of course, to ensure you are not tired, be sure to get plenty of sleep and rest. If needed, have some caffeine or take a brisk three-minute walk to get your body and mind alert and ready to engage the youth if the time for discussion cannot be put off until later.

By following this simple self-care plan, you can avoid *HALT* that will lead to the probability of engaging youth easier because you will have patience and compassion. Your mind will be clear, your body will be fit, your spirit will get well. This will result in a positive outcome for both of you, the adult and the youth.

*SOLER* is what the adult *needs to display* when trying to engage difficult youth. I found this technique from the author Egan (1986), to be effective when working with youth: **s**it squarely, **o**pen posture, **l**ean in a little, **e**ye contact—but not creepy staring—and be sure to **r**elax. If you are relaxed, and display such posture, more than likely the youth will respond to you much better than if you appear anxious, for instance.

To help you relax, you can think of that phrase "Red SOLER cup. I lift you up." Or sing the song in your head if it helps you to get relaxed when you are ready to talk to the youth. Of course, an alternative to singing, since I am not a singer, is what I use. I have found that for me personally, taking three deep breathes, inhaling through the nose and exhaling through the mouth slowly has assisted me in decreasing negative vibes like anxiety and stress. The result is that I know I will feel more relaxed and I know that this is needed when I am engaging difficult youth of today. All these techniques send an inviting message for the youth to be engaged and to talk or share their story with us. So be sure to use as many of them as possible and maybe find another one that fits your lifestyle if it helps engage, connect, and possibly even save youth! I know these work because not only have I used them, but some of my students have also reported that they are able to engage others better when they are *not HALT* and when they *are SOLER*. Therefore, you too can be successful in engaging youth when you approach them without HALT and with SOLER, and of course, a little PCT!

The implementation of these ideas into action should automatically display an approach to the youth as: Mind clear. Body fit. Spirit well. This approach, in turn, results in engaging youth of today as they tell their story to you! Just listening and simple nonverbal communication, such as a head nod or squinting the eyes as well as the 'uh-huh' or 'oh' gives the youth the cues to go on and tell you more of *their story*.

Now let's turn to the next section which is the action phase of engaging youth and where you can practice these with others or in the mirror if you are too self-conscious. Remember, have fun with practicing and then begin to use them with the youth you want to engage.

# ACRONYMS OR MNEMONICS AND ACTIVITIES TO DO THAT WILL ASSIST YOU WHEN ENGAGING YOUTH

In this section, you will find some acronyms or mnemonics, as well as some activities that will help you to begin and hopefully continue to engage the youth you are trying to reach and connect with. You may choose the activity that is the best match for the youth you are trying to engage then you may continue to use these ideas to maintain the engagement and further the connection between you and the youth. Remember though try to have fun with the activities while you practice looking in the mirror or role playing with another adult before you present this to the youth! You need to, at least, *appear* competent and confident, as well as approachable if you want to engage today's youth and connect with them. Also, recall that you need to approach the youth on their developmental level, so feel free to study the various theoretical stages of development that were highlighted in the tables at the beginning of this book.

## 3/Run HOMER

Each session that you have with the youth should cover the following topics with a male, but please note that it can be used for females, as well as other gender identifying individuals.

Below, you will see *3/Run HOMER* and how to use this technique as you begin to engage.

This one is beneficial for professionals since they assess youth and should cover each of the areas in this acronym during their sessions. Specifically, you should cover home life, medical and mental health, education, teaching techniques for success, and review, as well as offer positive reinforcement including verbal praise or a small token reward.

This specific technique can also be used by laypersons and is not only for professionals. Either way, remember to show a little PCT and open your discussion with open-ended questions to gather more information and improve the likelihood of your successful engagement with the youth. Ask the youth, "How do you think things are going?" (Open-ended question used here and pause to allow for further disclosure.) Follow up with specific areas at this point by stating: "How are things going at

- *h*ome (behaviors, chores, relationships in home only…),
- *o*pportunity (to use the skills taught since last time and actually used them or just *o*pportunity to do a good deed for someone or make a positive encouraging comment if no skills were taught to the youth. We are trying to reinforce any prosocial behaviors which are lacking today),
- *m*edication (compliance, changes, side effects, appointments) If not prescribed medication then *m*edical health (includes vision, early periodic screening, diagnosis and treatment [EPSDT], dental exams, *m*ental well-being),
- *e*ducation (behavioral issues, peer relationships, academic needs, individual education plan [IEP]),

- *r*eview of homework/assignments/skills/safety plans since last session,
- *3/run r*einforcement for good behaviors/using new skills,
- *r*eassign tasks/techniques as needed, and
- *r*eassess strategy during each session.

*Note*: A *3/Run HOMER* because no one is perfect all the time so a grand slam is not expected!

You can sing "Take me out to the (insert youth's name) ballgame. Take me out to the crowd…" Make the song your team song collaborating with the youth to strengthen your engagement and connection. This allows you both to be creative and lighten up with some fun. We know that fun creativity increases likability! Then the likability factor will likely increase the probability of engaging the youth you are trying to reach and connect with!

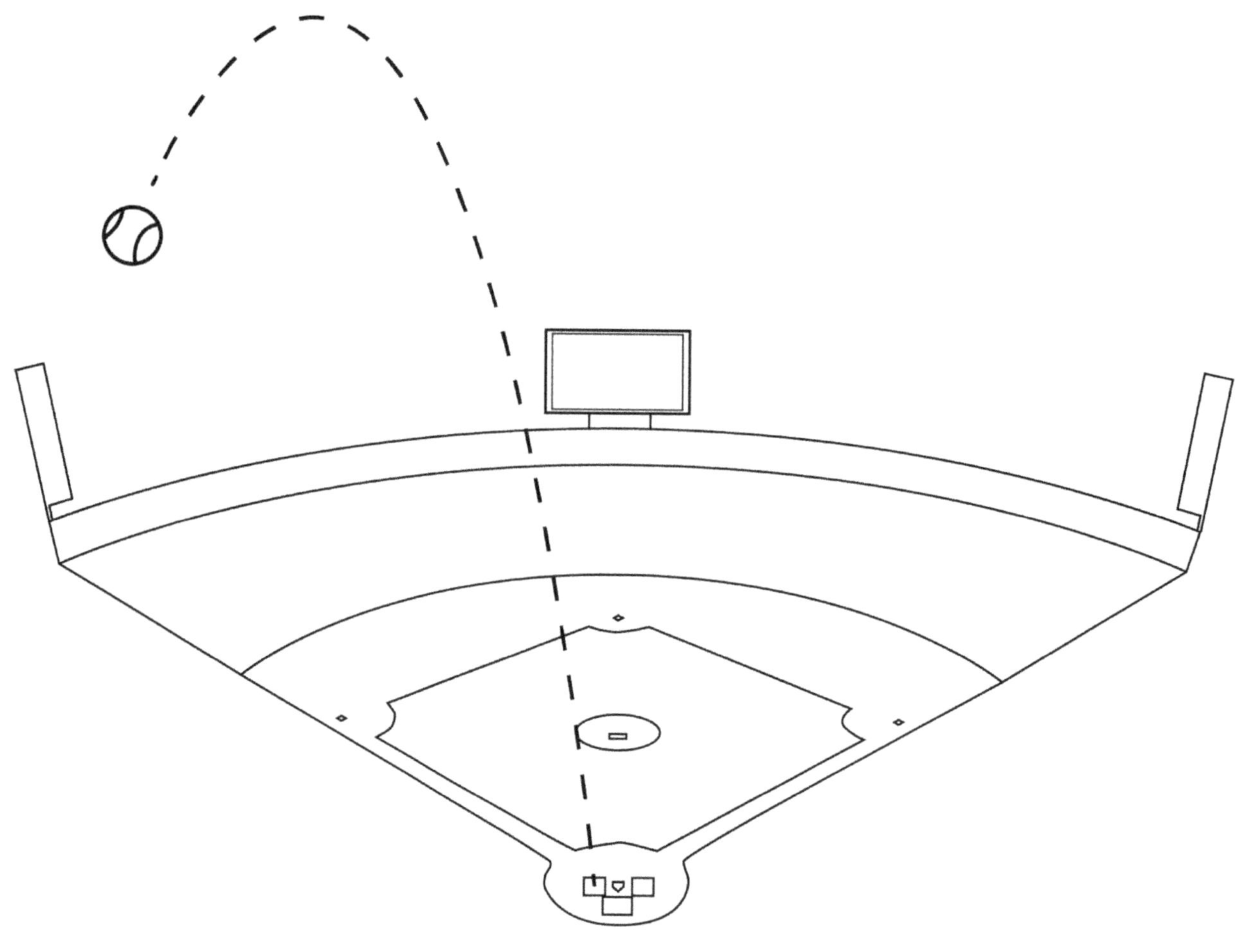

# 1, 2...3 RUN HOMER

# CHEER

Each session that you have with the youth should cover the following topics with a female, but please note that it can be used for males, as well as other gender identifying individuals.

Below, you will see *CHEER* and how to use this technique as you begin to engage. This one is really beneficial for professionals since they assess youth and should cover each of the areas in this acronym. Specifically, you should be sure to review skills taught since the last time you met by asking the youth if he or she has had a chance to use the skills, or if this is the first time using this, you can assess for how they have used certain skills in the past and if they would be willing to learn a new skill.

Also, *CHEER* covers home life, medical and mental health, exercise, education, teaching techniques for success and review, as well as offer positive reinforcement, including verbal praise and even small token rewards. This technique can also be used by laypersons and is not only for professionals. Either way, remember to open your discussion with an open-ended question to gather more information and improve the likelihood of your successful engagement with the youth.

Finally at the end of your session, be sure to reassess and wrap up to ensure that the youth understands what is expected between the end of this session and the next one you schedule. Begin by asking the youth: "How are things going?" (Open-ended question begins the conversation. Remember to pause as necessary to allow for the youth to disclose more at this time.) After the youth responds, ask them: "Have you had a

- *c*hance to use the skills taught since last time and actually used them?" (or just a *c*hance to do a good deed for someone or make a positive encouraging comment if no skills were taught to the youth. We need to increase prosocial behavior amongst the youth of today so if they respond in the affirmative, then praise, praise, praise them for being prosocial.) Then ask them how things are at
  - *h*ome (behaviors, chores, relationships in home only, etc.);
  - *e*ducation (behavioral issues, peer relationships, academic needs, individual education plan [IEP]);
  - *e*xercise and health (medication compliance, changes, side effects, and appointments). If not prescribed medication then include vision, early periodic screening, diagnosis and treatment [EPSDT], dental exams, mental well-being;
  - *r*eview of homework/assignments/skills/safety plans since last session;
  - *3/Rounds (of cheer) r*einforcement for good behaviors/using new skills;
  - *r*eassign tasks/techniques as needed; and
  - *r*eassess strategy during each session

You can even develop a *CHEER* together that is encouraging and reinforcing positive behavior. This can be co-cheerleading to strengthen your connection with the youth. Make it your own team *CHEER* collaborating with the youth to strengthen your engagement and connection. This collaborative activity allows you both to be creative and have some fun! And we know that creativity that is active and fun increases likability!

As a result of this light-hearted and fun interaction, the youth and you can increase connectivity with each other! Youth will begin to engage the adults that they like. Likability is your super adult power so use it to help!

CHEER!!!

# CHAT(S)

Each follow up session should cover the following topics for any youth that's breathing! Specifically, this technique I call *CHAT(S)*, is used when the youth exhibits negative behaviors such as yelling, cursing, rolling their eyes, not listening, kicking, or hitting, as well as many more undesirable behaviors. This acronym can be used at the beginning of an engagement session during the middle of one or at the end of a session. *CHAT(S)* can occur in the home, office, grocery store, automobile, train, plane…. you get it. Quite frankly, anywhere and everywhere negative behaviors can occur, *CHAT(S)* can too! Just be sure to have some privacy as to not embarrass the youth in order to maintain engagement and connection that has already been established.

Now the *S* pertains to *safety*, so at times, a *CHAT* may have to occur in front of everyone, especially if there is no time to pull the youth aside for privacy or due to safety issues the *CHAT* must occur swiftly and without delay. For instance, a child running into the street after a soccer ball without stopping and looking. This is impulsive and is a safety issue, so a *CHAT* needs to occur immediately!

I have used *CHAT(S)* throughout my career and have found them to be quite rewarding. I always begin with the youth's name because this is what gets their attention. You want to be sure the youth is listening to you before you begin your CHAT which is meant to be a dialogue using PCT and even SOLER when possible.

At times, HALT may be present due to having to engage in a CHAT quickly because of a safety issue. If the CHAT could be delayed a little or you need to calm yourself however, remember your go to relaxation and anxiety reduction techniques. Again if there is a safety issue, then address this immediately and without delay. State the youth's name and be sure that he or she is listening. Then softly repeat the youth's name again and state (youth's name here). We need to have a *CHAT* because I

- *c*are about you, and although I
- *h*ate this negative/hurtful (describe the attitude or behavior). I really do
- *a*ccept and like you as a person, so I'm going to
- *t*each you a new skill, so you are able to (offer rationales for new goal) (If safety is an issue, add the *S*.) and
- *s*afety is very important. This little *CHAT* we had will also ensure *s*afety of all, including you.

Be sure to have the youth repeat what you have stated so they cannot use the statement, "I did not know or understand what you said last time." If the youth did not comprehend then have another CHAT and get verbal feedback to ensure the youth is receiving your message.

Here is an example of *CHAT*:

The adult states, "I *c*are about you and I *h*ate your yelling at your brother. I *a*ccept you as a person and I want to *t*each you to use an inside voice because it will keep you out of trouble (rationale for learning new behavior offered), and you will be liked by other people because you will not be seen as being annoying (another rationale offered for using new skill). Let's practice using an inside voice (model the inside voice for the youth)."

Encourage the youth to use the inside voice and offer positive reinforcement for doing so. This simply means give the youth verbal positive feedback and encouragement. Also, later, catch them being good as they use their new founded skill. By praising the new behavior you taught, the youth will likely increase using said skill which automatically results in decreasing the negative behavior of yelling inside the house at the brother as in this example shown. Also, the *CHAT* permits you to maintain engagement with the youth when *SOLER* is used as you spread some PCT, so be sure to include this posture and this tone at this time. Feel free to use this space for writing your own example of a CHAT or CHAT(S) between you and a youth. Practice a couple CHAT(S).

# CHAT

## ART

Each session should cover the following topics for all youth if you have not chosen another acronym to use during your time spent with a youth. This one is beneficial, I have found any way, for youth who are artistic. They like *ART*, and this is a way to check in with the youth in a nonthreatening fashion. Again keep it simple and light always focusing on the positive in order to continue to engage and connect with the youth you are serving.

Get the youth's attention by stating his or her name first. When the youth looks at you or, at least, in your direction then repeat their name a little softer and state while using *SOLER* the following:

"It's time to have *ART* class. We start by having an

- *a*ttitude check that is ready to
- *r*eceive feedback based on what I just heard (or observed). Now let me
- *t*each you really quick, and then you can try again by *t*eaching me so I know you are capable of (the skill or having a positive attitude)."

An example of *ART* might be an adult asking: "How's your attitude? Good, fair, poor, horrible, or what? Describe your attitude for me please."

Youth responds.

Adult asks, "Is your attitude ready to receive some feedback or comments based on what you told me?"

Youth responds positively.

Adult states, "I'll teach you, and then you teach me. For example (youth's name here to get their attention), you said you had a bad attitude because you failed your math test. That's all right to feel bad when you fail a test, but it is not all right to have a negative attitude toward others who had nothing to do with this issue. So teach yourself and challenge your negative thought and negative behavior or attitude by telling yourself, 'Yes, I failed a test, but it is not the end of the world. I am still alive and breathing and I have a choice to keep this bad attitude or let it go and move on doing better on my next test. I will be more positive even when a minor setback occurs because I do not want this negative attitude to cause me to have *dark ART* work where others will see it and not want to look at my *ART*. I want people to see my *ART* talent and that I can overcome minor setbacks and have a positive attitude. I will make my *ART brighter* rather than dark and gloomy which others do not want to see, including me.'"

Then get the youth to reframe their *negative ART* work into a positive and offer praise as positive reinforcement when they try to teach you the skill of *brighter ART* work.

Discuss the difference between dark ART and bright ART with the youth. (Obviously some youth will like the dark ART anyway so you can still process this with them through discussion on their cognitive developmental stage to ensure they are grasping the meaning of ART.)

- ➢ Have the youth draw gloomy ART work (dark colors only) and/or draw bright ART work (bright colors only).

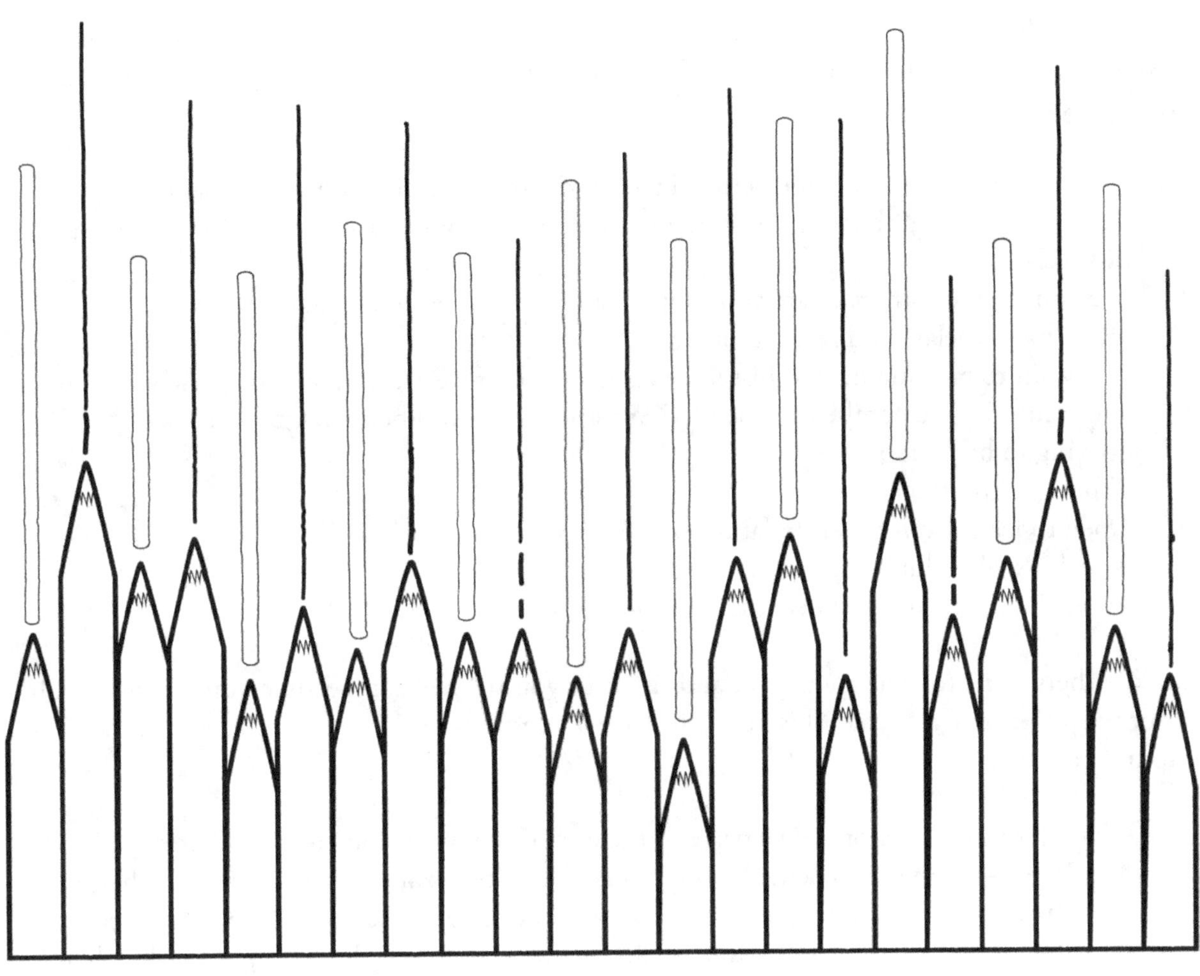

## STORY or STORI

Every youth has a *STORY!* We need to stop and listen to hear *their* unique *STORY!* You can ask the youth for their *STORY.*

There are a few ways to use this technique. For instance, if you want to get to know more about the youth, you might ask, "What's your *STORY?* Would you be willing to tell me about your life *STORY?*" Specifically, ask the following:

- Do you *s*trive to be someone better? Hero or doctor or athlete? Or what exactly?
- *T*ell me something that only your best friend knows about you that makes you who you are unique or special.
- Are you *o*pen to others or are you more of a guarded or even closed off person?
- How do you *r*elate and *r*eact to others?
- *Y*ou want to be remembered just like everyone does if we are honest with ourselves, so tell me how you want to be remembered. Your *STORY* is how you will be remembered.
- *S*triving to be better;
- *T*alking with others;
- *O*pen to learn from others' relationships and;
- *R*eactions when hurt, sad, or mad. All of these are how
- *Y*ou will be remembered because it is *your STORY!*

Make others want to read about you and listen to you so they can become your friend and be proud of you (or whatever may motivate this youth to have a good *STORY!* For example, stay out of trouble, get closer to my parents).

- ➢ Write or draw your story (Five pages at the end of the book. One for each letter—STORY!)
  - ▪ Page 1—Striving to being better. My goal is to be (example: a doctor or teacher or what?).
  - ▪ Page 2—Tell something special or unique about you. (Example: I can draw well.)
  - ▪ Page 3—Open to share. (Example: A picture of two people sharing candy or chatting about something important.)
  - ▪ Page 4—Relating to others and reacting to situations. (Example: Pictures of sad, mad, glad, scared.)
  - ▪ Page 5—You are being remembered. (This is a totally blank space so the youth can project on the paper how they really want to be remembered.)

Then read *their STORY* or go through the five pages and discuss their story! Each of these can be on its own page so the youth can be creative and write *their STORY* like writing a booklet. Then they can create a title page that shows who they are as a person and staple all six pages together to have their own booklet which is *their STORY!* Let the youth know that they can rewrite *their STORY* any time they feel they need to make improvements because they are in charge of their outcome no matter what they have been through or are going through.

There is hope for a positive outcome to their story if they choose one! Remind the youth that by engaging and connecting with a trusted adult, *their STORY* can have a happier ending! When the youth and you are working on this topic together, be sure to remain engaged with the youth. Be sure to encourage them whenever they make a small positive step toward completing this task. It is important to use small verbal reinforcers of encouragement. This task may take a couple of sessions which is ideal because the youth can continue to modify their work. Be sure to use open ended questions to further discussion. Also, be sure to implement PCT which will more than likely keep the youth and you engaged furthering a positive connection built on established rapport and mutual trust. Let the youth tell *their STORY* because this is about them at this point.

Another variation of *STORY* might be something like this below:

- S—How are you *striving* to be better?
- T—How can you *talk* to others?
- O—How can you be *open* to learn from others?
- R—*Reactions* to *relationships* which made you sad or mad or where you were hurt.
- Y—How will *you* be remembered in *your STORY*?

(I have used this for assessment of youths before. I look for any signs of being hopeful in the present or having a hopeful ending. If there is no hope presented by the youth, I needed to address depression and even suicidal ideation. If this negative issue is noted by you, be sure to seek professional help immediately for the youth if you are not a mental health professional. Also, address any other negatives throughout the story written or drawn by the youth.)

A third way one may use *STORY* is to get the youth to remember *their STORY* themselves by asking them to tell *their STORY* each time when they are making a decision. In other words, it is a decision-making tool that may assist youth in staying out of trouble. It must be taught through modeling by someone (the adult) who is willing to tell a little about their own *STORY* when he or she was younger. Also, *STORY* must be applied and reinforced consistently by the adult for it to be effective. Here's an example of how to apply it when a youth is having difficulty with making good decisions:

> Youth acted out because she did not get her way and was told "No!"
>
> Adult asks, "What's your *STORY*? Your actions are telling me a *STORY* that I really do not want to remember. I would like for you to tell me a different *STORY*, one that is much more pleasant because this is how I am going to remember you and want to remember you when I think about you.

This is something I used when I was about your age, and it really helped me be remembered in a more positive manner. I told my *STORY*! I said to myself

- *s*top!
- *t*hink about my
- *o*ptions so I can
- *r*espond appropriately so
- *y*ou're remembered as doing well (for example, behaving, helping others, playing nice, or cleaning)."

Here is an example so you may practice telling *your STORY* in making good decisions!

➢ Below, example of child or teen area to tell his or her *STORY* or *STORI*! I am going to tell my *STORY* now! Before I react in anger or self-harm or (other negative behavior) I say to myself
  - *s*top,
  - *t*hink about my
  - *o*ptions so I can
  - *r*espond appropriately so
  - *y*ou're remembered as. (Actually, you can change this last one to "*I* will be remembered as a youth who made a great decision and put smiles on the faces of people I care about! So here you can tell your *STORI*, but you know it is *YOU* as in *STORY*!")

➢ Write your *story* here. (S-T-O-R-Y is located on pages 72–76 of this book for easy access and copying. Also, you can include in the youth's STORY pages 78–80 on Mind Clear. Body Fit. Spirit Well.)

# FOLLOW UP SESSIONS

The uses after each acronym or mnemonic are only *suggestions*. Feel free to use them for other issues as well.

WISHED

WISHED or BE WISED can be used for a discussion about educational issues.

When working with youth, you need to have a sense of humor albeit warped and odd at times…well, most of the time to relate to and engage many youths.

*Education* is important in the world in which we live today. There are many who struggle with getting youth to complete their school work. Unfortunately, the dropout rate is still pretty high. So if education is valued in a family, then the likelihood of dropping out will be lowered. Rather than lecture about education, you might try having *WISHED* that your youth would value education.

Here, you can use a silly or odd voice with an expression of curiosity when you present the importance of education to the youth. For instance, one may say in a higher pitched voice than normal or a deeper voice or even a silly cartoon character voice (or whatever voice you know your youth likes to hear other than the lecturing voice because that gets tuned out by youth, so please do not use *that* voice!).

As an example of this approach, you may state with sincerity yet curiously and being in a playful mood. "(State child's name to get attention), I *WISHED* for you today (name again). [Having the attention and their curiosity continue.] What I *WISHED* for you today was that you

- *w*ork on your school assignments
- *i*ntelligently and
- *s*tudy for your quizzes and tests
- *h*ard in order to earn your
- *e*ducational
- *d*egree.

That's what I *WISHED* for you today. I did this because I care about you and your future!"

No matter what the reply, you—the adult—must smile and wink and ignore any negative behavior. Repeat this exercise daily and use positive reinforcement no matter how small the progress!

There are a couple of alternatives that you could use for this *WISHED* exercise, of course. For example, the first way is BE *WISED*, or specifically, to use *BE WISE* and earn your *d*egree. (The humor can be found in *wise* versus *wised*, and if the teen calls you on your grammar, smile and say you have *WISED* up so continue to study and *BE WISE*!) Keep it playful to maintain the engagement and open doors for what may become good discussions not only about education and their future educational goals, but current issues may be impacting their education. In particular, maybe the youth is not doing well in school due to some issue but is embarrassed to seek out assistance or to disclose that they have trouble reading or writing. Yet when you maintain engaging the youth, you can get to know him or her and assist them in confiding in you to get the resources needed to help with becoming wise and educated.

A second alternative is to use *BE WISE* above and add "earn your education or earn your GEd." Just remember to use an odd or silly yet curious voice, and the youth will begin to see that you're not a stick in the mud and maybe you really do care and that you are sending a gentle message that she or he needs to care as well. Obviously, this is done through the adult modeling and using positive reinforcement every time the youth is on the correct path. Remember, catch them being good, and if at all possible, ignore the negative.

You can also remind them of what Nelson Mandela once said, "Education is the most powerful tool we have to change the world" and even share with them how your education has helped you change your world or the community in which you reside. Likewise, you may share with the youth that you know how different athletes or movie stars have used their education to help others in need!

WISE

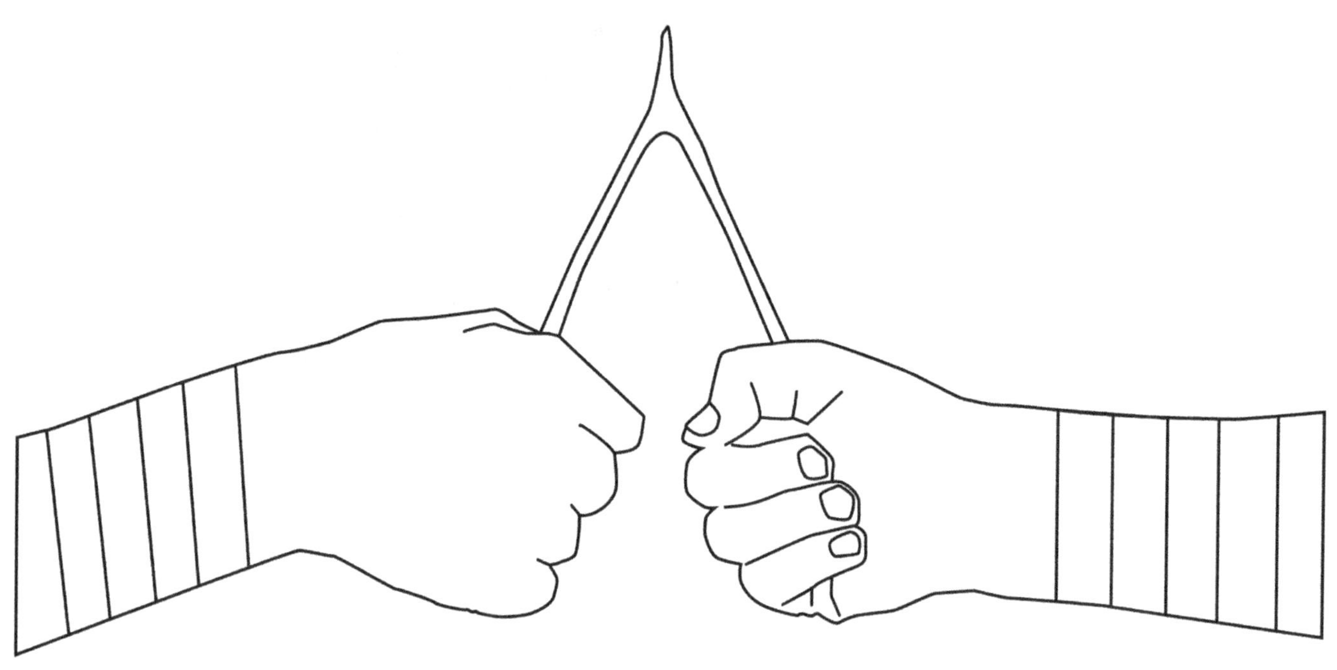


WISH

# BRAIN

BRAIN can be used for decision making, planning, and minimizing impulsivity. Please remember to always begin an exercise with the youth's name to ensure they are listening.

I find it interesting that God called the prophets by name on most occasions twice. If God said, "Moses, Moses" or "Jacob, Jacob," maybe it is important to use a youth's name twice. Besides, a connection begins when we use someone's name. Don't you feel special when someone you meet for the first or second time is using your name in sentences when they speak to you? I know I do! It is great to be called by one's name. So try it!

Try using the youth's name at least twice when speaking to them. Keep in mind the gist when using this technique "Are you using your *BRAIN*? If not, please use your *BRAIN* power. You are so capable of doing so, (youth's name). By using your *BRAIN*, you can be more successful in all that you do!"

Here, during this interaction, the adult uses *BRAIN* by stating something like the following:

- "How are your *b*ehaviors this morning (day or week or specific situation)?
- Did you accept *r*esponsibility for your
- *a*ctions (or lack of *a*ction)?"

*Who* or *what* could you (or did you) *i*nclude to assist you to improve in this area and to be successful? (Or if they were successful, *who* did they include or *what* did they do? And can they *i*nclude the same person or the same action to be successful or even improve some more?) I wonder what *n*eed(s) are (or *n*eeds are not) being met by this behavior and by using (or not using) your *BRAIN*?

An example of when to use this might be when you have a youth that is not doing his chores. Specifically, he only has to take out the garbage one day per week and seems to forget to gather the garbage from his bedroom and the bathroom, but he always remembers to get the garbage from the kitchen area. This is what the interaction might look like between you and the youth when using *BRAIN*:

- How did you do with the garbage this morning? (How are your *b*ehaviors this morning, specific situation?) [Youth responds that he forgot to take trash out from his bedroom.]
- Whose responsibility is it to remember to get the trash from all the rooms? (Did you accept *r*esponsibility for your *a*ctions (or lack of *a*ction in this case)?) [Youth responds, "It's mine. I just forgot."]
- Who or what could you *i*nclude to assist you to improve in this area and to be successful? [Youth states, "Maybe I could set a reminder on my phone or write a note on the refrigerator."]
- I wonder what *n*eed is being met here by forgetting. Any ideas? (Need(s) are (or are not) being met by this behavior and by using (not using) your *BRAIN*?) [Youth classically states, "I don't know. I think I forgot. I won't do it again."]
- All right, so you are going to remember because you are going to use all your *BRAIN* next time because you came up with a couple of good ways to solve this issue. Let's set the alarm on your phone now or let's get that note you suggested written and placed where you will remember next week. Sound good? [Youth replies, "Yes." He then goes and does it.]

Of course, you need to be sure to check that this is completed. Assist as necessary to ensure it is done correctly. Do not be sarcastic or facetious when discussing *BRAIN* with the youth in order to avoid losing the connectivity you made or even disengaging them all together rather be sure to praise the youth for using their *BRAIN* instead! Remember, a little PCT goes a long way in relationship building and maintaining!

You can also discuss a little about the brain activity. We, adults, must remember that the prefrontal cortex part of the brain is not fully developed until about the age of twenty-five, according to researchers. The prefrontal cortex is responsible for executive functioning, such as planning, decision making, reasoning, problem solving, and even memory and regulating some behavior. This part of the brain assists with curbing impulse control issues too.

If a youth is suffering from ADHD or autism spectrum disorder, researchers have found that the area of the prefrontal cortex is different. This means a little patience on our part as adults can assist in setting youth up for success rather than failure. Break the plan of action into baby steps if necessary.

When a youth begins to use that brain power, reinforce it. Again typical youth will *forget* which means that we adults must be patient and use continual reminders to ensure their success.

> ➤ Label four parts of the brain. Frontal lobe, temporal lobe, parietal lobe, and occipital lobe. Draw a picture of the new behavior and how it will be accomplished here.

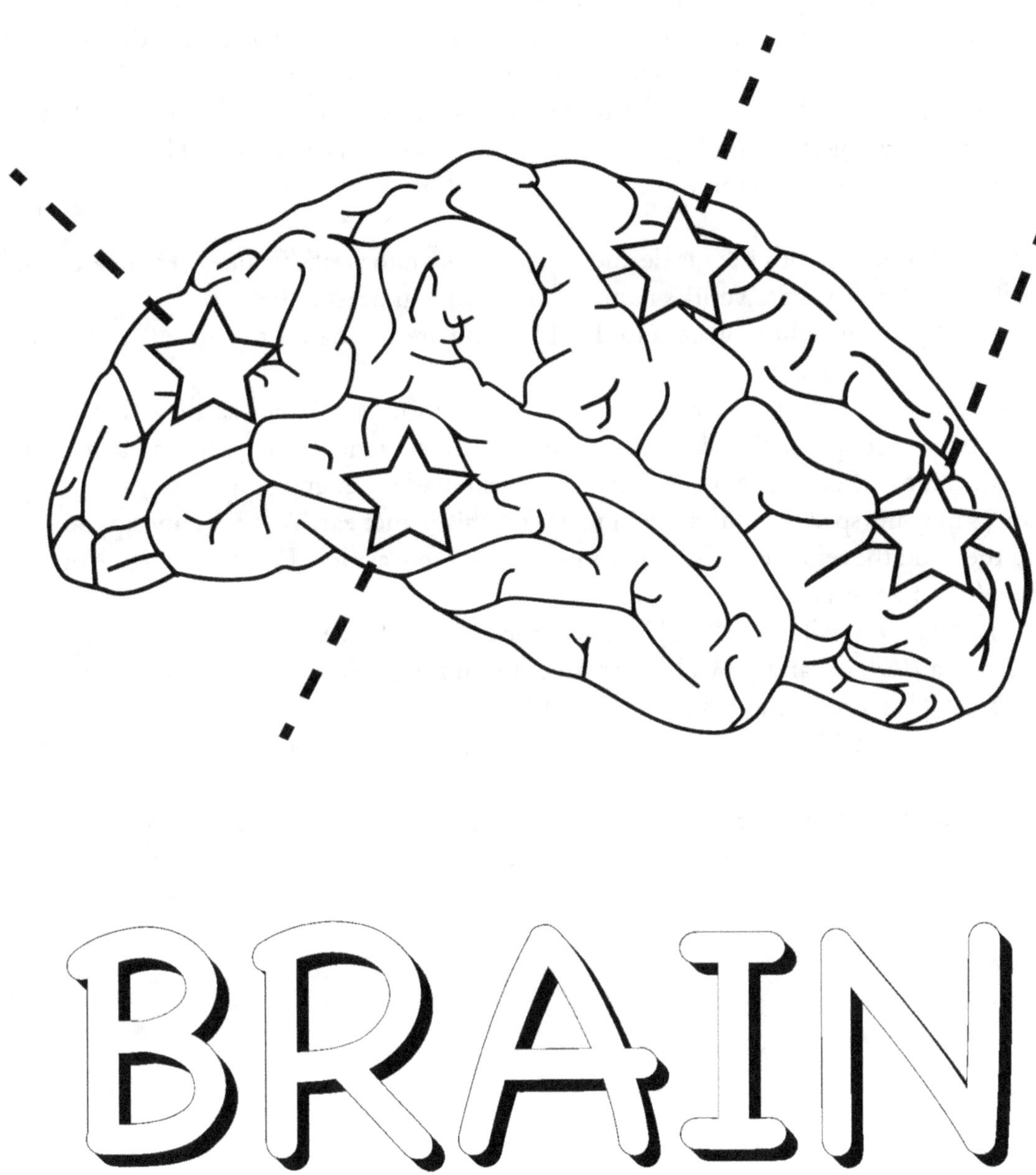

# BEACH

BEACH can be used for a youth with low self-esteem or for a last session with them.

"Have you ever been to the *BEACH* or have you ever seen pictures of a *BEACH*?"—this is the question you might ask a youth when you need to engage one that you know has low self-esteem. Quite frankly, that means pretty much any youth that you might encounter. You can refer to the developmental theories discussed in the beginning of this book, especially Erikson's psychosocial crisis of adolescence.

Do you remember when you were a child, or especially a teenager? It was quite awkward many times, wasn't it? So you might go to the *BEACH* to not only accomplish engaging the youth but to also assist in building their self-esteem! Who wouldn't want to accomplish both these tasks?

The outcome is going to be beautiful for all involved because as you and the youth talk, you can imagine being at the *BEACH* together forming a positive connection with each other! Here's an example of how the adult can introduce *BEACH* to the youth:

- *B*eauty is found on both the inside and the outside (state youth's name). There are many beautiful qualities about you (state youth's name again), and you need to be
- *e*ducated on them right now because I believe you are too hard on yourself! You have made quite a few
- *a*chievements in your (specify youth's age in years) on this planet earth! For instance, (you, the adult, name a couple achievements and then add the sentence) I bet you can name a couple as well! [Youth can name one or two here.] You have also made so many good
- *c*hoices in your (specify youth's age in years) on this planet earth! For instance, (you name a couple and then add the sentence) I bet you can name a couple as well! [Youth can name one or two here.] Therefore, I am very
- *h*opeful that you will do well as you make the correct choices throughout your life. I mean, after all, life is a *BEACH*, and we will either sink or swim. I know you will enjoy the swim though since the *BEACH* is a beautiful place to be free! Don't you want to be free from negative feelings and negative thoughts? How can you be free from this negativity and feel better about yourself?

By asking this open-ended question, you will more than likely further your discussion which affords you the opportunity to engage more through a good dialogue involving positive reinforcement and praise!

# BASKETBALL

BASKETBALL can be used for positive praise of youth's positive attitude or behavior. This technique involves the adult asking the youth something like "Do you…

- *b*elieve your (or alternatively, begin by stating), I *b*elieve your
- *a*ttitude was
- *s*uper
- *k*ind (or cool with a *k* as in *kewl*),
- *e*specially
- *t*oday!
- *B*elieve this
- *a*ttitude is a
- *l*esson
- *l*earned for us all!"

Ask what the youth's thoughts are on this and then practice how to safeguard it continues—for example, you might inquire, "What lessons did you learn from your positive attitude you showed?" (He or she was liked by others, received positive praise from others, earned more freedom to do more or whatever the positive outcome was as a result of playing *BASKETBALL*.) Reinforce the idea that being good at playing *BASKETBALL* is a learned skill, and the more one practices, the better one becomes and eventually masters the skill. This applies to mastering positive attitudes and behaviors as well.

# BASKETBALL

# PILOT

PILOT can be used for when the youth is doing well and positive reinforcement as well as teaching "I" statements to the youth. The adult begins the conversation on a positive note because this sets the stage for engaging the youth. If the adult begins with a negative tone, the engagement process is limited if not deleted.

*PILOT* can be used as a teachable moment and to reinforce whatever positive behavior has occurred. The adult can state their thoughts or even ask the youth for theirs depending on whether the adult is pleased or not pleased with the youth's actions.

You know the drill by now; begin with the youth's name here, then ask:

- *P*—Are you *p*leased with your behavior? Please explain a little about your *p*erception of your actions. (After the youth responds, either agree or disagree with the "I" as follows):
- *I* am or *I* am not pleased because (using an *"I" statement*** and encouragement to continue or change behaviors while maintaining respectful engagement of youth).
- *L*—What can be *l*earned from this incident? I'm always here to listen.
- *O*ptimism is what we will focus on because I believe in you. More importantly, you need to be optimistic so you can… (Describe behaviors or actions, as well as thoughts that can improve and become positive thinking to succeed.) This will, in turn, teach and/or tell.
- *T*—teach others and *t*ell *your story* about how you overcame this behavior. You were the *PILOT* who flew away from the negative behaviors and thoughts and you landed safely in the positive!

Point out how people look up to and respect leaders and those in uniform, including PILOTS.

**A word about *I statements* which can be used as a teachable moment. "I" statements have three parts: begin with the pronoun "I" followed by the word *am* and then add a *feeling* and finally describe the *behavior* without judging the youth. It looks something like this: "I am feeling frustrated because the shoes were left in the hallway and dirtied the floor I just cleaned," or another example of an "I" statement might look like this: "I feel very happy that your report card showed several *A*s and *B*s this time, as well as many satisfactory grades for behavior." Even if there was a grade of *D* and an unsatisfactory for a behavior, notice that there is no judgment, and the focus is on the behavior and not the youth being bad or not as smart or motivated to achieve. Using "I" statements will increase your chances of maintaining the engagement and connection established between you and the youth thus far.

By maintaining the relationship, the adult will be able to continue to be a role model for a youth who learns to trust the adult because he or she has a caring attitude toward the youth. You can return later and discuss how the youth might be able to improve the *D* grade, as well as the unsatisfactory behavior grade. Again focus on the positives if that is what you want to see increase in the near future. Besides, some youth suffering from conduct disorder will not respond well to punishment or threats trying to cause them fear. Also, children suffering from oppositional defiant disorder (ODD) will argue about everything, so the best way to handle this is to give choices. This is how you win an argument with a youth who is ODD. You give them a couple of reasonable and realistic options and let them choose. Their choice will allow them to think that they have the power, but in truth, you still get what you want and without an argument and a stress headache.

Thus, focus on the strengths of any youth no matter if they have a mental disorder, learning disability or are just stubborn!

# PILOT

# KING

KING can be used for focusing on the present (emotions and issues), not past negatives.

- *K*eeping
- *it* in the
- *n*ow is
- *g*ood.

You can talk to a male youth about being a *good KING* by focusing on the present and not digging up past negative events. The adult might state something like this: "If you want to be a *good KING*, you need to keep it (your emotion) in the here and now, the present, because it shows you have control, which is good.

Here's some reasons why I *myself* (referring to you, the adult) am seen by others as a *good KING*, and you can be a *good KING* too! People will see you (insert youth's name) as a *KING*. What do you think of when you hear the term *KING*?"

Wait for the youth offers his responses, acknowledge his comments, and continue with "If I am *KING*, I am less likely to be set off by old triggers because I am *k*eeping *it* in the *n*ow—the present—which is *g*ood! I don't let negative behaviors from the past take control of me" or "If *I* am *KING*, I'm more likely to get a kind response or some information from the person I am talking to."

(Here, we are trying to engage the youth more, so you are king in this situation!)

"As king, people are likely to pay attention to us if *we* are *KING*."

(Here, the youth will observe your nonverbals so you will have to keep them in check. Notice the change from "I" to "we" here for establishing unity and collaboration purposes between you and the youth.)

"When you are *KING*, you are likely to decrease escalation between you and others, such as, in this case, between the adult—that's me and the youth—which is *you* (insert youth's name here)."

(Notice the change again: *we* to *you* which now places ownership on the youth.)

Finally, being *KING* increases compliance, and you get what you want more often than not. Remember, a *good KING* gets a *good QUEEN*, if that is what the youth wants now or in the future.

KING

## QUEEN

QUEEN can be used to focus on emotions and connect on an emotional level.

- *Q*uietly
- *u*nderstanding
- *e*very
- *e*motion
- *n*ow in the present.

After reading the *QUEEN* approach above, you might be wondering what it will get you from the youth you are trying to engage and reach.

- First, it will assist you in obtaining more information from the youth. We may feel uncomfortable dealing with silence.
- For me, however, I was able to sit with the youth for a period, and eventually the talking began. Your face has to show interest, not boredom, distraction, frustration, or anxiety. Those displays on your face will probably shut the youth down, so always, and I mean always, avoid displaying those looks and giving off negative vibes. Also, do not show intense emotions like you want to take control instead just relax your body and be patient in silence. Yes, you remember "Mind clear. Body fit. Spirit well"? Now put these into play here!
- Second, by using *QUEEN*, you will earn some respect, or as my Latin youth would state *respecto*. This earned *respecto* is important to youth, for without respect, you will gather no information and remain disconnected and unengaged with the youth.
- Third, by using *QUEEN*, the youth will have the belief that you care because you are not forcing them to talk and you are patient as they gather their thoughts of what to share. It may be quite difficult for a youth to share their thoughts with you, at times, a stranger, so show them that you value them by sitting still for a bit in silence.

  You can encourage them to talk after a couple of minutes by simply asking them, "I'm curious, what are you thinking about right now? I really do want to hear what you have to say. If you need another minute to gather your thoughts, please feel free to do so. I am here to hear you out. You have a story, *your* story to tell, and I am listening!"

In doing this, you might see the youth test with no comment or reaction or even a rude verbal or non-verbal display of action. But you need to chill because this will allow you to gain something very important to further your relationship, which is finally more trusting. And through more trust, you will gather more information needed to engage the youth in a healthy manner. Remember, queens get kings or other good things.

This technique is a good way to discuss the basic emotions as well. We all get mad, sad, glad, and scared. You could ask the youth to share a time that they were mad and process what happened before, during, and after they were mad. Likewise, you could take each of the other basic emotions and do the same line of questioning and processing.

This has worked for me over the many years, and the youth tend to like discussing their stories about the four basic emotions or feelings.

At times, though, a youth had a history of being traumatized. As a result of some youth being traumatized, they may not want to discuss an emotion, like getting scared. Therefore, you can ask them to return to scared at a later date when they feel safer to talk about it.

Also, this may be a sign that a youth may need professional assistance if they are not involved with a counselor yet. Do not overreact and demand that a youth tell you every emotion or feeling because this is a roadblock to communication and ultimately stops the connection to the youth. Remember, the goal is to engage the disengaged youth, so be patient with the process. Queens get kings is what you need to remember! You can say something like "By us two sitting here *quietly*, we can *understand* *every* emotion *now*. I want to focus on the present and how you feel. But I also want to discuss your past emotions as well. Please feel free to share, and I'll quietly try to understand you."

# TRACK

TRACK(S) may be used for decision making skills or apologizing to someone.

At times, events occur rapidly, and we do not know why they do. They just do! It's like running a track meet or a fast race. Sometimes our brains just go so fast with thoughts, and we do not stop and think about what might happen until it is too late. (For example, a youth with ADHD or impulse control issues.)

In using *TRACK(S)*, the adult may begin by asking the youth to

- *t*rack a time that your brain was
- *r*acing so fast that it was hard for you to act
- *a*ppropriate for the situation (allow the youth to respond). Now what were the
- *c*onsequences you had to
- *k*eep even though you didn't want to live with them? (Allow the youth time to respond.)

After some responses from the youth, add the *(S)*…

- *Sorry* is what we wish we could say at times, isn't it?

Saying *s*orry and truly meaning the apology, whether or not those consequences would be removed, shows that you are running a race to better yourself and this, in turn, shows you are bettering the human race too. You can then ask the youth if he or she would like to apologize. After their response in the affirmative, you can continue by stating something like this: "You know (insert youth's name here), you can say you are *s*orry to this person by writing a letter even if we don't give the letter to the person. Being sorry can help you heal. If you prefer, you can draw a picture of how sorry you are if you do not want to write a letter," or "To win the race around the track involves taking ownership of your actions. Sorry is part of this process. The choice is yours. You can be *s*orry or you can continue to let your brain run around the track without ever making any progress and then all you are doing, is being the first loser. Since you're not a loser (youth's name), I know you will make the right choice now. You can choose to finish the *TRACKS* and be a winner!"

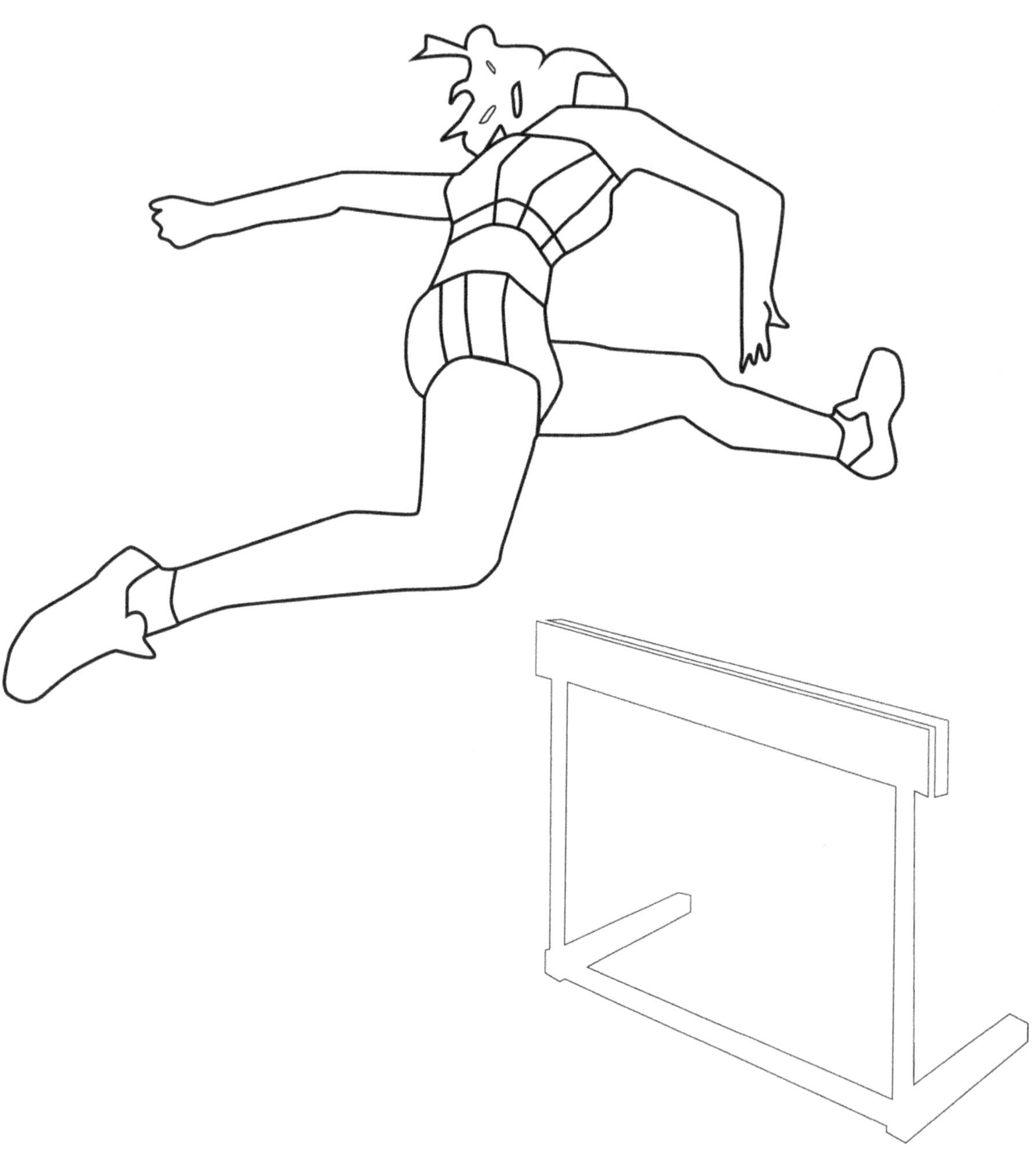

# TRACK

## SAPPY

SAPPY can be used for adults offering reassurance or empathizing with the youth.

Sometimes the youths have a very difficult day at school, and they are feeling stressed about their life. Maybe the youth failed an exam or didn't make the softball or baseball team or was bullied by their peers. When you see the youth hanging their head or moping around and you know they had a lot of problems at school or in the neighborhood even, it may be time to be a little *SAPPY*. Of course, you know by now. Start by stating the youths name to get their attention then say to the youth something like this: "I know, at times, I am a little *SAPPY*. (Be sure to smile here.) But I am truly

- *s*orry
- *a*bout the
- *p*lenty of
- *p*roblems
- *y*ou had (specify, for instance, today/this week at school/in the neighborhood/at youth group).

I know this can make you feel a little sad or down and troubled about your life." (Be sure to pause at this point. Look for body language that shows the youth is getting the meaning being sent by you.) Then continue with something like this here: "You know that I can be *SAPPY* at times, but I am here for you and I have had similar experiences like you, so I hope you feel like you could share what's going on. Here's a tree that has some sap dripping from it. Sometimes I feel like this tree too and maybe that's how you feel now… (Pause for reaction.) Let's color this tree and make it look better. I think we'll both feel better." (Using *we* to show that it is a team effort, done in a collaborative manner.

Also, it shows that the adult is feeling or empathizing with the youth. This, in turn, should lead to an increase in the youth's engagement with you and a move toward a closer connection, which is the goal.)

The tree here has some cuts and scrapes in it too to show it had a rough time. There may even be a squirrel hole to show that trauma may have occurred or there may be a tree without it and see if the child puts a hole on the trunk.

(*Note:* This does not always mean a trauma has occurred since many children place a squirrel hole in a tree bark, so do not panic. However, if you suspect any abuse, please ensure the youth is receiving treatment for his or her trauma from a trained mental health professional.)

## TREE

SAPPY TREE can be used by adults who are offering encouragement to share a part of their story. It can be used by trained professionals to assist a youth work through trauma. This technique can be used by any adult when discussing something bad that has happened to a youth. However, a bad incident might be a traumatic event and therefore would require a trained professional to help the youth work through.

Either way, the adult would start talking to the youth with *TREE* below only after using *SAPPY* first since *TREE* is a follow-up technique.

- *t*rying to
- *r*emember
- *e*verything from the
- *e*vent that is difficult, but it is important to discuss this because you will feel better eventually.

The adult continues after using *tree* above by stating, for instance, "I'm here to listen while you work on this picture of a tree with the sticky stuff or sap dripping out." If you are a trained mental health professional, especially if you are trained in working with youth on traumas they suffered, you might proceed like this after you used SAPPY:

- *t*rying to
- *r*emember
- *e*verything from the
- *e*vent that is difficult, but for you to eventually feel better, it is important to discuss the
- *t*rauma's
- *r*eminders,
- *e*motions, and
- *e*vent(s).

By discussing these, you will heal and become a survivor. The *r*eminders are the cognitions or thoughts that are associated with the trauma you suffered. The *e*motions are the feelings like mad, scared, sad, and even glad that the *e*vent is over. The *e*vent(s) involve the behavior or actions and is sort of like "fight, flight, or freeze." Maybe the *e*vent caused you to fight but the person was too big or you tried to take flight and get away but were unable to do so. Maybe you tried to fight and take flight, but you couldn't do either of those, so you could only freeze your body and had to escape in your mind to a safe place.

I hope you can begin to share with me the *t*raumatic *r*eminders, *e*motions, and *e*vents little by little so we can work through them together knowing that you are not alone, and that there is hope as other youth have made it through *SAPPY TREE*s before. They are survivors and you can join the rank too!

Let's color this tree here while we talk.

The tree can be copied and used for each season. Let the youth add to or just color as he or she wishes while you talk together. Do not lead the youth in any direction as he or she is working on their coloring. You can ask them which season they think they are in and be sure to discuss this on their cognitive level (Piaget's cognitive stages as discussed earlier in this book), not their chronological age since these are not always in sync. Then during your next session, you can show them their tree they colored and ask them if they want a new one to color representing a different season of the year or if they want to continue working on the same tree they started on. Let them have control here since they were not in control of the traumatic event. You can let them know that if they color all the leaves brown then they will fall off and eventually new leaves will emerge representing new life and a new beginning as they work through their trauma and troubles.

This is what you want to see—a youth who is positively changing. Focus on their strengths and all their positive qualities. Even if a youth takes brown and black colors only and marks up the tree illustration, this is progress. This shows you the possible hurt and depression they are experiencing.

Over the next couple of sessions, encourage the youth to add some color representing that they are changing and becoming a survivor.

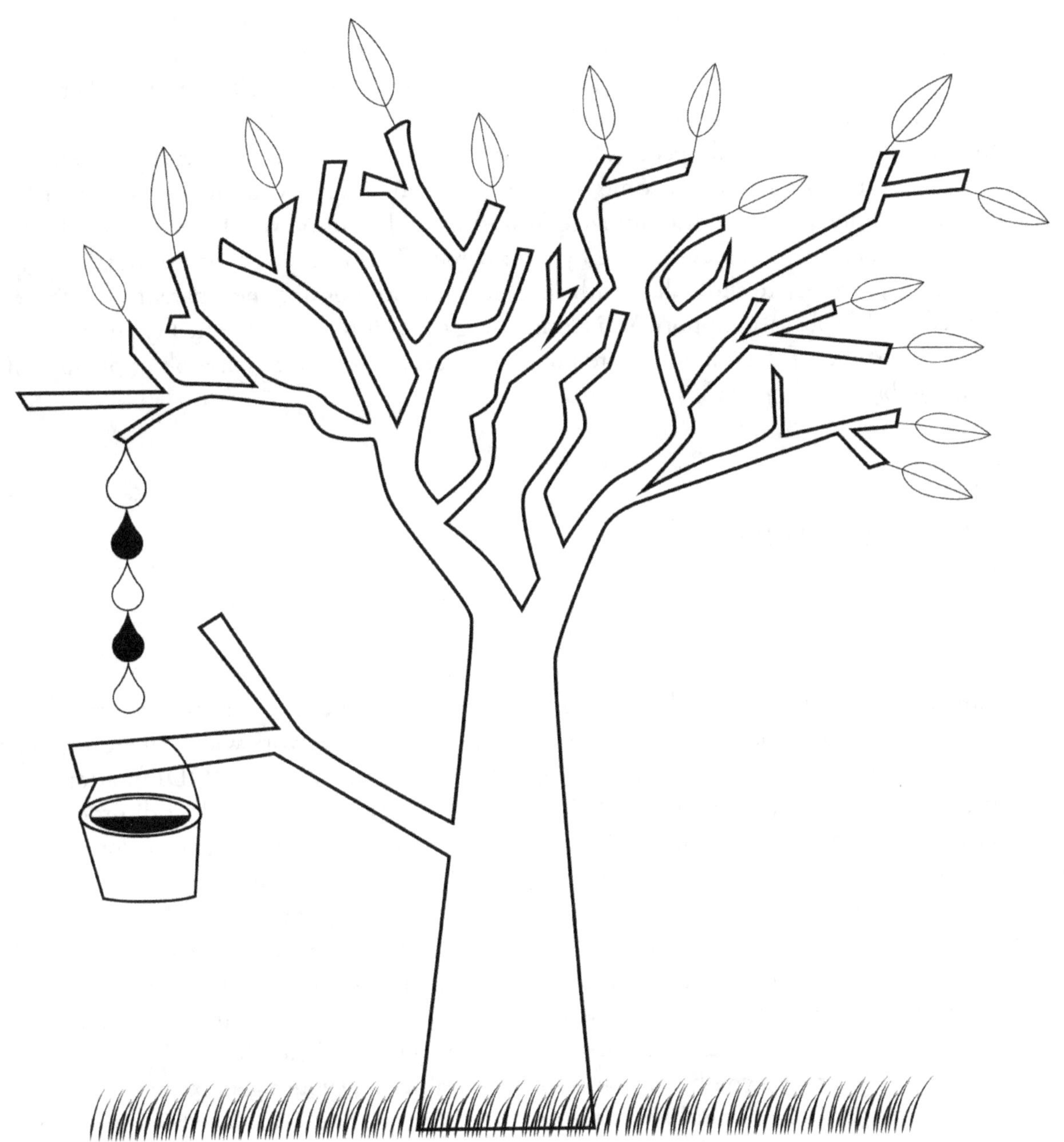

# SAPPY TREE

# CRUISE SHIP

CRUISE SHIP may be used for discussing autonomy or equality and power differences.

The adult needs to think what it is like to be on a *CRUISE SHIP*. They are huge!

You are such a small part of that cruise ship. The youth, too, is only a small portion of that cruise ship. It is easy to get lost as you move throughout the ship and visit the different decks.

The ship has a history and so do people. The youth, like you, has a history with preferences or likes and dislikes. The ship has been through some rough waters and so have you and the youth. There were times when a youth felt inequality or discriminated against and a loss of power. The youth has been treated unfairly—for example, maybe they were abused by their parent. This is not only unfair, but wrong.

You have the opportunity to show the youth that all adults are not like their parent who abused them and can be trusted to offer positive support. You are assessing the youth's sense of equality and need to gently confront their irrational belief that all adults are not to be trusted. You both can look at pictures of cruise ships to remind you both to be able to

- *c*ome to a
- *r*ealistic
- *u*nderstanding of (the youth's)
- *i*ndividual
- *s*ense of
- *e*quality.

The youth already understands the difference in power and will, of course, test the waters for the power differential between the two of you. There may be youth that you know or work with that are argumentative because they are suffering from a mental illness of oppositional defiant disorder (ODD), attention deficit hyperactivity disorder (ADHD), mood dysregulation disorder, may even have conduct disorder, or because they are suffering from another mental illness. Maybe the youth does not have a mental disorder but is simply oppositional on some days. Really, which youth does not argue on occasion?

Either way, you can share with them that you are on the cruise ship together, and they do not have to be alone on this huge ship in strange open waters. Tell them to trust you because you are present with them and you want to connect with them. State something like "Could you please *s*hare *your h*istory and *your i*ndividual *p*references (likes and dislikes)? Because I want to know more about you as we cruise through the waters in this huge cruise liner together. Trust me, I won't let you go overboard."

This works well if you have a youth that wants to take a cruise. The youth gets excited and begins to tell you what they would like to do and not like to do. You can get a lot of information about history and individual preferences during this time so be sure to ask open-ended questions and use positive reinforcement when the youth shares with you part of their story.

Their history includes their family (biological or foster or adoptive), educational changes and transitions experienced, and any other area they want to share about. Their preferences are a part of their story, so ask about their hobbies, how they like to be treated, their friends, and even their perceived enemies, as well as their tastes in food and athletics or any area that gets you and the youth more engaged and connected to each other.

The hope is that they will see the trusted adult is the captain of the cruise ship and for now, they are the passenger. As they mature, and move through the developmental stages (e.g., Erikson) they can become a cocaptain and eventually become the captain of their own *CRUISE SHIP* as they make good choices.

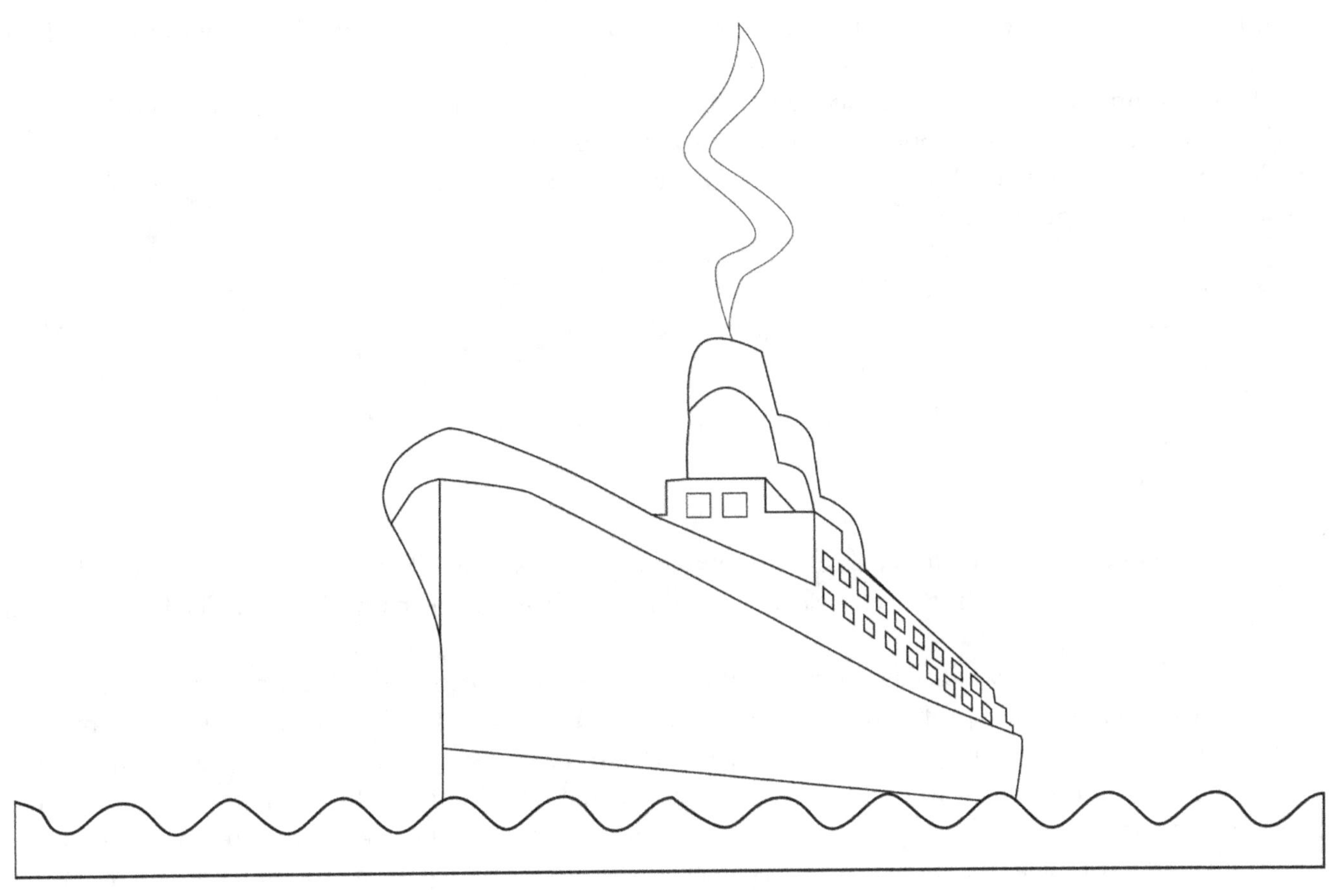

# CRUISE SHIP

# TENNIS

TENNIS can be used for discussing any disclosed or suspected abuse of youth.

Any type of abuse is very difficult to discuss with youth. It is important that when a youth discloses any type of abuse, whether physical, sexual, or even emotional or psychological, adults report this disclosure to the proper authorities. In addition, if there is suspected neglect (for example, not meeting medical needs, educational needs, or basic food and water needs), a report must be made to the local child protective services or social services agency or call 911 if necessary. If disclosure occurs about any abuse experienced by the youth, you need to get the youth mental health assistance so a professional may work with the youth on healing.

This is a long process. However, any adult that has a meaningful relationship with the youth can use *TENNIS* to talk to him or her about their abuse they mentioned.

When a youth hints or directly discloses that they have been abused or neglected, you can say, "Let's play an imaginary game of *TENNIS*—

- *t*ell
- *e*veryone
- *n*ow!
- *N*ow we
- *i*mpede
- *s*ecrets!"

In other words, "(State youth's name), we do not keep secrets. We tell other adults to get the assistance needed to heal and be well. Hit the tennis ball and tell me more about the painful secret. The ball is in your court."

Again, if the youth does discuss more detail and you are not a professional, do not pry but get them connected to a mental health professional. The youth told you the secret, maybe only parts of it or maybe the whole story, but either way, the youth trusted you enough to tell you some secret and the ball is now in your court to hit it to a professional to deal with in an effective manner. By doing this, you are letting the youth know that you are being supportive and that they can trust you to care and take action to assist the youth.

You should also be a role model, which is what youth of today need. You are modeling for them that keeping dirty secrets is not acceptable and only causes more harm than good. You can also model that is acceptable to state "I do not know why this bad incident occurred." This lets the youth know that bad things happen to even good people, and we do not have the reason why they do but that they do. By stating you do not know, you are modeling telling the truth which will give you credibility here. By doing so, you will more than likely gain cooperation and maintain the engagement and connection you made with the youth.

Finally, during this difficult conversation, be sure that you will do everything you can to protect them and keep them safe. Do not promise that this will never happen again though because unfortunately we cannot guarantee that it will not. Therefore, only promise and reassure them that you are going to do everything you can to ensure their safety from now on.

Also, thank them for sharing and tell them how brave they were for telling you a part of their story and that they can tell it again to a trained professional.

It is an utmost importance that when using *TENNIS*, you are *not HALT* and you are using *SOLER*. Be sure to do no harm is what every adult needs to keep in mind. To be sure you are doing no harm, you need to be in the here, and now with the following being displayed: Mind clear. Body fit. Spirit well.

If you are unable to follow these guidelines, you will do more harm than good which will result in a disconnect between the two of you. You may even cause the youth to disconnect from other adults because they may think that because of what you did or said or did not do or did not say, other adults will let them down as well. This only reinforces their belief that adults cannot be trusted. They will remain with their emotional pain and are then set up for attachment issues that will continue later in their adult life.

Again, be sensitive to the youth's issues and be sure to maintain healthy boundaries, only doing good in order to maintain the connectivity established.

Finally, be sure to talk to them on their cognitive level, recalling Piaget's levels of cognitive developmental stages that were presented earlier in this book.

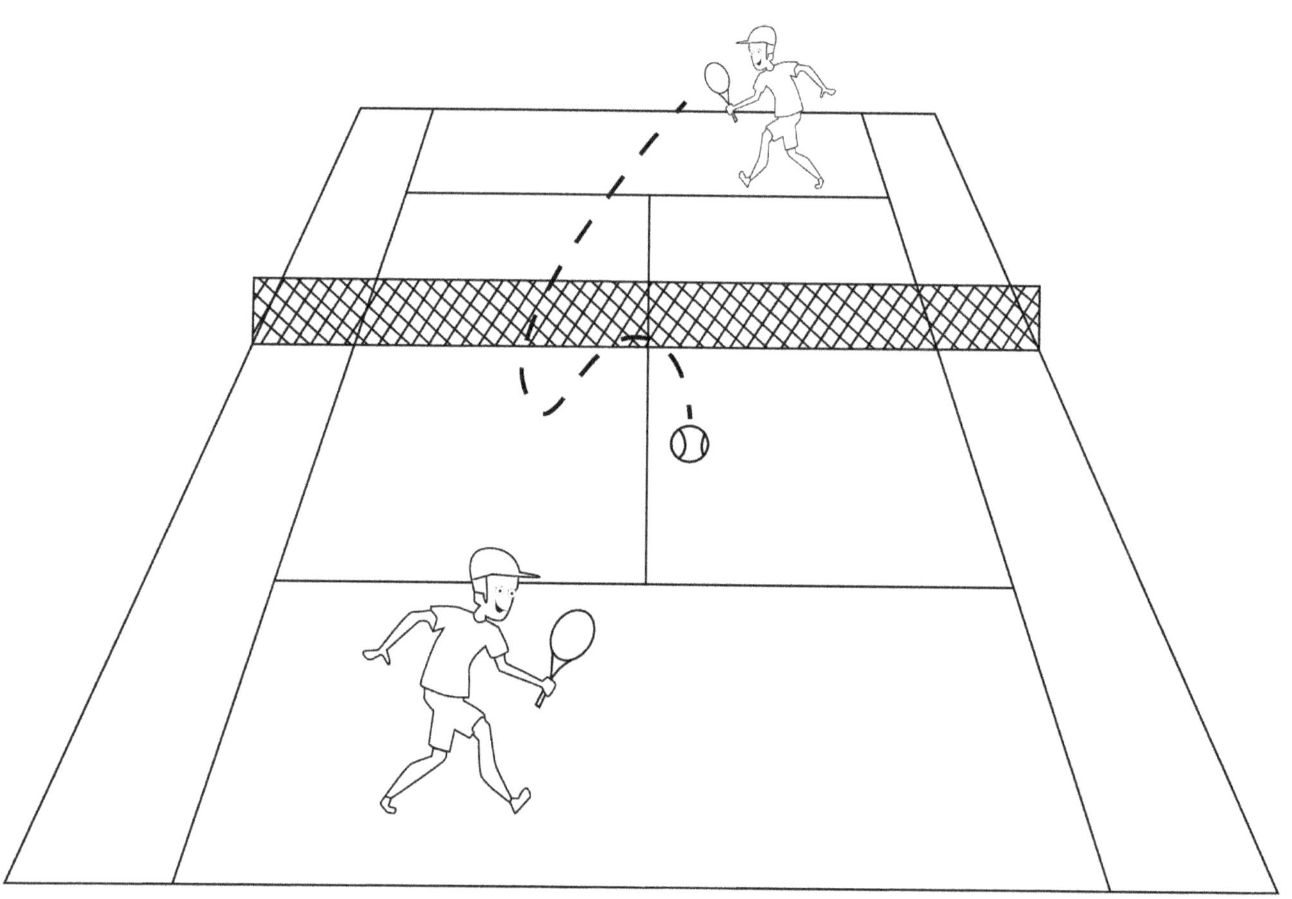

# TENNIS

## GOLF FOUR

GOLF FOUR can be used for learning from past mistakes and failures.

When the youth confides in you that they messed up, you can use *GOLF FOUR*. Start this conversation by stating that you appreciate them sharing that they messed up and invite them to share more about what happened. Remember that you can sit with the silence for a little while to allow the youth to gather their thoughts. You then explain that you have to *GOLF* sometimes! You can say something like "You have a

- *g*reat
- *o*pportunity to
- *l*earn from
- *f*ailure and messing up (or mistakes).
- *F*ailures are
- *o*pportunities to make it and
- *U*
- *r*ight."

Then discuss what the youth can do to make it right. You might say, "(Youth's name), you admitted to messing up, and if it is all right with you, I will be your caddie (the golfer's experienced assistant) and assist you in learning to make it right with the person (or thing) you offended (hurt or whatever fits the youth's issue of *messing up*)."

This might involve paying compensation, doing extra chores, or stating or writing an apology, promising not to do it (say it) again. You and the youth can role play the *o*pportunity to make it right to correct a wrong if possible! Praise the youth for any positive outcome to increase the likelihood of positive behaviors occurring in the future.

Also, reassure the youth that they can share anything with you to fix the issue. Let them know *your* story of *GOLF FOUR*! This is a good way to be a role model and to give them an idea of how to make a wrong right, as well as let them know that there is hope in the future. We do not have to become our mistakes. We can and all do grow as long as we learn from our errors.

FOUR!!!
GOLF

# RELIGION AND SPIRITUALITY

The topics of *religion* and *spirituality* are difficult topics to discuss with youth, especially teens at times. Some teens proclaim to be agnostic, pagan, or even atheist as they are forming their identities. However, most teens do believe in some form of *spirit* or a *higher power.*

To discuss religious or spiritual beliefs and values with the teen, the adult needs to begin with a non-judgmental attitude by utilizing active listening skills by asking a teenager why he or she believes what they do warrants; a strategy that maintains mutual respect and the right of the youth to choose their belief system, even if you, the adult, may be upset, angry, or shocked by what you hear.

The reality is that the teenage years are times for being oppositional and even defiant as they strive to form their identity and become autonomous. This struggle for independence from adults may involve the youth going in the opposite direction of what you have taught them or what they have been taught by other mentoring adults. This covert or overt rebellion from the youth may be a very sensitive area for the adult as you have mixed emotions and feelings about your own child or a youth that you mentored or are mentoring now.

It is not easy to instill values in a youth and to see them challenge what were taught them even though we all did this to some extent during this time. However, it is imperative that the adult remain calm and follow the simple steps if communication is to be maintained and the relationship is to be mutually valued.

On the next couple of pages, you will find *RELIGION* and *SPIRITUALITY (SPIRIT)* acronyms that you can learn *prior* to your conversation with the youth. You might find these helpful as they have worked for me to get into the minds of youth and their thoughts on these topics. You can also refer back to Fowler's stages of faith development discussed earlier in this book and try to guess at what stage the youth you are talking to might be.

No matter how you approach the youth on this topic, be sure to keep an open mind and a poker face on to keep them talking and stay engaged! It is so important to make a connection with youth on a spiritual level so be sure to not shut them out or down!

## RELIGION

- *Respect.* To appreciate, what the youth is sharing is important. They are expressing themselves, and we must listen in order to build rapport and a positive relationship. Pseudo-relationships exist when there is no respect or *respecto.*
- *Expectations need to be discussed.* For instance, attending synagogue, mosque, or church needs to be addressed even during this identity formation. They must follow the rules of the home or state law as applicable (e.g., in foster care and their age may matter). If it is expected that the youth attend, then they need to do so or consequences need to be implemented.
- *Listen intently.* This means we are not on our tablets or cell phones or being distracted by other items or other people. We are looking at and reflecting and paraphrasing what the youth is stating during this time. Asking for clarification when we do not understand allows the youth to know

that we are invested and are listening because we care about what they have to share. Include *SOLER* in here but do not include *HALT*!

- *Individual belief of youth is valued.* To value does not mean to agree. It means that you see the youth as having some worth. You are showing that you care that the youth is becoming an individual and unique person. This is a chance for you to model valuing others' opinions even if you do not agree with them. Be sure to thank them for sharing their values!

- *Give positive reinforcement only.* Show some positive reinforcement for allowing individuality as long as the youth is respectful toward others as well. If it is difficult to even say, "Thanks for sharing your thoughts" then it is best to smile and give a slight nod showing that you heard the youth's thoughts. This must be sincere though if you desire to maintain engagement and establish a deeper connection with the youth! Offering positive praise for their sharing will increase more sharing later on and even a deeper, more meaningful connection with the youth.

- *Interest in further dialogue must be shown.* The best way to show interest in further dialogue, at times, is to simply ask. For instance, you might ask, "Can you share more on that thought? I really want to understand what *spirit* means to you." Again, focus on the positive! Do not argue at this point unless you want to disengage the youth. They may not talk to you as much later on if you challenge them right now, so just listen. A discussion or debate has the intent of changing another's mind, so dialogue is done in respect and with the intent of understanding where another is coming from. Thus, stay in dialogue at this point, and maybe if you feel it necessary, you can playfully engage in a debate at a later date if the youth would like to do so. Many do because they want to prove the adult wrong. At times, debate is healthy as discussion is. However, I implore you to stay in dialogue here to maintain open communication and engagement.

- *Openness to the youth's current beliefs on religion should be maintained to keep dialogue open.* The quickest way to shut a youth down and to not see any progress is to be closed-minded. Again, being open to what the youth has to share about what they believe keeps the dialogue alive, and you will get to know the youth and what they value. Commonality can build stronger connections since as the saying goes, "Birds of a feather flock together!" Try to find any commonality between you and the youth no matter how small!

- *Never judge nor you too shall be judged.* Remember, judging is a roadblock to communication and will draw criticism toward you. Best practice then is to not ridicule, mock, insult, minimize, nor demean any thought related to spirituality that the youth has shared.

You may want to read my dissertation if you are working with an older youth or young adult in college. I have included the reference at the end of the book in the references section in case you want to research it further (Sapp 2011). Remember, the Bible is clear about judging, and we are all fallible human beings.

# SPIRITUALITY (SPIRIT)

- *Sincere.* Being genuine and honest or straightforward is a must when discussing this topic.
- *Present in the moment.* Focusing here and now is where your mind needs to be. Yes, do not be *HALT* because you will not be in the present but rather focused on a deficit that needs to be fixed in the near future.
- *Intensely listening.* This is a form of active listening. This is where you, the adult, will use the *SOLER* technique and have the body language that speaks louder than words. This is where you need to put on your interested face and attentive body language. The youth is watching what you do very closely.
- *Respecting their belief system.* Even though you may be shocked by what you hear from the youth, more than likely, they are just testing you and looking for a reaction, so it is in your best interest to let the youth know that you respect their right to their belief system even if you do not believe in it. Save your comments to vent to another adult so that you display a respect for the youth's belief system which will maintain the dialogue. If you vent to another adult, do it in private and far away so eavesdroppers do not hear what you are saying. Overheard sidebars are quick ways to lose the youth's trust and result in disengagement and mistrust down the road.
- *Interest in further dialogue.* One way to do this is to use slight head nods or cues for the youth to tell you more. For instance, you could state "Uh-huh," "Hmm," "Okay," or even "Please share more on that point." Be sure to nod your head and have eye contact but not staring the youth down as "I dare you to go on with this nonsense! Spiritual aliens?" or you will shut him or her down and may never have the opportunity to learn about their spirituality again.
- *Teachable moment.* This is important! If you have a *true story* from your personal life, you can share it here and apply it to the youth's story. Try to tie it in to what they have just shared with you and not to *one up* them or belittle what they just shared. When in doubt, there is no reason to share a story until you have had a chance to share it with another adult. At this time, if you are not going to share a teachable moment, you can tell the youth that you plan on returning to this topic and hope to share a little about your spiritual journey since they were able to share their thoughts on this topic. For me, I have some interesting beliefs that youth hold to that differ from tying various religions together to far out outer space beliefs involving the spiritual side of humankind. Either way, no matter what you just heard, always tell the youth, "Thank you for sharing your personal values and spiritual belief system with me. I appreciate you letting me know you better and look forward to more good conversation and sharing." This is a great opportunity for modeling appropriate dialogue, which currently seems to be a rapidly fading art in our globalized world.

To get this conversation started, you may say something like "I am *s*incerely interested in your thoughts on spirituality and want to be here right now, in the *p*resent, *i*ntensely listening and *r*especting *your* beliefs about spirituality. I'm *i*nterested, so please share with me, and maybe we can *t*each each other about our views" (then use *SOLER*).

➤ Draw religious and/or spiritual beliefs here.

➤ Comment about what you believe here. It can also be one word or short-written phrases that explain youth's beliefs.

# SAPP

SAPP may be used as a clinical note or documentation in your personal log or journal.

Whether you are a professional or not, documenting your clinical note or personal note about your time with the youth is important. I always teach my students "Document! Document! Document!" That's how important this part is for you and the youth.

If you are in the helping professions, such as nursing or counseling and psychology, you have probably heard of a SOAP or DAP note? Here, I introduce you to my original *SAPP* note because I think it is important to have alternatives to what is out there already for documentation purposes.

In addition, this can assist you in recalling who wrote this book! I have times where I could not recall the author of a book I read when I was explaining some concept of a book before. Maybe it's my age, but it is a little embarrassing for me anyway not to remember the author.

So this new *SAPP* note will not only assist you with remembering how to write a good note and document your intervention well, but it will allow you to recall quite easily who wrote this book about Engaging Youth of Today: Mind Clear, Body Fit, Spirit Well.

In *SAPP*, then the *S* is for *Subjective*; *A* is for *Assessment*; the first *P* is for *Problem*, and the second *P* is for *Plan*. This is like subjective, objective, assessment, and plan in the SOAP note.

In a DAP note, the *D* takes on the subjective and objective in the SOAP and is confusing to some as reported by some of my students, both undergraduate and graduate alike.

But since I wrote this book, I thought of a new way to recall how to write a clinical note or again a personal note you can remember and tuck away in a safe place. Here is an example of a *SAPP* note where I am writing about a youth named Johnnie who has come in for a follow-up counseling session due to aggressiveness at school.

- *(S) Subjective*—Johnnie reports that counseling is not helping as much as he thought it would. He insists that he is managing his anger well but then reports not using the STOP technique taught to manage his anger. He then reports that he had a physical altercation with a peer at school. He states, "When I get angry, I lose control because I saw my stepfather doing it." (*Subjective is what the client or person is reporting to you.*)
- *(A) Assessment*—Johnnie appears to be minimizing the severity of the fight at school based on the medical report relayed by the PE teacher. It appears he is making excuses for his anger, blaming his stepfather. However, Johnnie does report honestly that he did not use the STOP technique. (*Professionals would then include some of the mental status exam [MSE], as well as their professional opinion for a diagnosis.*) Johnnie is disheveled, presents with flat affect, is alert and oriented to person, place, time, situation. Rule out oppositional defiant disorder (ODD).
- *(P) Problem*—During the session, we continue to address anger management by role playing using the STOP technique. We also practice through role reversal and discussed through talk therapy (Socratic dialogue therapy), rationales for using anger management techniques, and how they can assist him in obtaining his goals of managing his anger and staying out of the principal's office.
- *(P) Plan*—Schedule next session for (*specify date and time*) to continue to work on anger management skills. Johnnie practices his breathing exercises twice for two minutes each day until our next session. Next session, will follow up with homework given on breathing exercises and introduction of another technique to challenge irrational beliefs client has via cognitive behavioral therapy, such as Rational Emotive Behavior Therapy or REBT.

Signed (*with credentials for professionals*) and dated.

Once your note is documented, it needs to be locked away safely. It is mandatory for professionals with the youth's information to ensure the confidentiality of documents by having them locked behind two locked areas. Likewise, it is important for laypersons to maintain confidentiality for the youth they are mentoring or serving by keeping written notes locked away and not left out in the open for anyone to read. If confidentiality is broken, unless required by law to break confidentiality as in disclosed abuse, your connectedness will be diminished if not eradicated by gossip or being lax with the youth's trusted information. Do not betray their trust that they have in you! Protect their disclosures that you have documented in a safe place.

The next time you are getting ready to see the youth, you can pull out your clinical or personal note and review it so you know what you are to do while meeting with the youth. You can begin with a *CHAT, CHEER* or any number of exercises in this book to get you started with your session and maintain the engagement you already made with the youth.

It is very important to follow-up with the youth about any homework you assigned because if you do not, it shows you do not value homework and then they are less likely to do it in the future. If I had a teacher who did not collect nor check my homework, I would not complete it, would you? I sincerely doubt it because there is not a reward for doing the assignment. Besides, there are so many other fun distractions like playing outside or video games.

In this situation regarding homework, the reward for completing the assigned task can simply be positive reinforcement. In particular, Johnnie can be praised when, in the example shared in the *SAPP* note, he reports that he did not have a fight at school, and he used the relaxation techniques during the week. Then you can practice exercises assigned in session and offer positive feedback as well.

You may even have a small reward for the youth if your budget allows it. Again, this should be small or you will go broke rather quickly. In addition, the reward should be small or the youth will begin to always expect a tangible reward and may not complete homework tasks if he or she knows there is not going to be any payoff for completing the task, like money or a king-sized candy bar.

Praise really does go a long way, so use your smile and positive words which do not cost a dime!

# CONCLUSION

One time, I worked with BA and her family doing home based services. I was teaching the technique called *timeout*. I recall discussing in detail, the rationales, for using timeout and how to implement and enforce it in their home. I asked the parent if she had any questions, and when she did, I answered any questions she asked. What I failed to do was go through how timeout should *not* be used. Even though I did say don't use the bathroom or kitchen for timeout because they are dangerous areas since there are knives or medications in those rooms which can be used to harm a youth. I did not, however, say that a child should *not* be placed in a closet.

This was a *teachable moment* for us all and was quite humorous, at least, and not dangerous as it might possibly have been in another home.

So always review and practice with a minor or adult when teaching a skill. Also, be sure not to judge but rather review if we, the adult, are to blame first. We need to assess: did we teach everything right? Did we leave any steps out? Does the youth truly understand what we are teaching him or her?

In this situation with BA, it worked out for the good because at six months follow-up with her and her mother, BA was placed in time out in the hallway as agreed by all parties, and only needed it twice.

It is also important to remember not to judge or label resistance until you investigate yourself (a self-analysis) and what you may have done wrong, including whether or not you omitted something. Use teachable moments for both you and your youth you work with or youth you may be raising yourself in your own residence. It is best to step back and show no emotion on your face, and then if safe to do so, leave and return to the situation later when you can maintain your composure. If needed, use another adult as a sounding board to bounce ideas off and get feedback.

You can even practice some of these techniques with another adult, or again, use a mirror to assess your body language. The goal is to not overreact but to only act calmly in order to gain trust and to ensure you are maintaining a positive relationship to build a better tomorrow full of hope for all involved in the relationship.

Granted these encounters with youth may have setbacks as time goes on as in any relationship. Be mindful of this and stay focused on the positive, as well as any progress you've made with the youth. If you sense that the youth needs more assistance than you can provide, whether you are a guardian, biological or foster parent, or even a professional, be sure to obtain the necessary trained professional help for your youth. And remember, the sooner you can get aid, the better off all will be.

Finally, if your mind is clear, body is fit, and spirit is well, I do believe you will engage with and connect to, at least, a couple of youth in your life. You have planted the seed, and even though you may not get to watch the youth mature and grow as much as you would like during the time you have with them, my experience tells me that many youth do indeed recall that you tried to engage them and steer them on the right path.

As teens or young adults now, they do appreciate your attempts and, of course, successful engagements. I have been told this and I am sure some youth will find you or run into you somewhere in this world and tell you thank you for helping them be a better person. Without your attempts to connect, they would have remained disengaged and in their pain. So don't give up on the disengaged youth because if every adult reaches out to just one youth to assist or to mentor, that youth will, in turn, remember and begin to assist other youth throughout the lifespan.

# STORY (S)

Page 1—Striving to being better. My goal is to be… (Example: a doctor or teacher or what?)

# STORY (T)

Page 2—Tell something special or unique about you. (Example: I can draw or sing well.)

# STORY (O)

Page 3—Open to share. (Example: A picture of two people sharing candy or chatting about something important to them.)

# STORY (R)

Page 4—Relating to others and reacting to situations. Divide the paper into four and draw the emotions. (Example: sad, mad, glad, and scared)

# STORY (Y)

Page 5—You are being remembered. (This is totally up to you—project on the paper in words and/or drawings of how you really want to be remembered by others.)

# Mind Clear. Body Fit. Spirit Well.

These next three pages are for developing your plan for having a mind that is clear, a body that is fit, and a spirit that is well. Draw and/or write your plan of action on the next three pages that you can use to accomplish the task of being healthy. Keep it simple and remember you can always add as you find something new that might work for you or you can delete something from your original plan when you find that is not working for you. The important point is that you need to have a plan in order to maintain a mind clear, body fit, and spirit well when making a connection and when telling your story to others. You can ask the youth to complete these and add to *their* STORY.

There are so many options for a mind that is clear: meditate, pray, deep breathing, nature walks or gardening, putting your smartphone down, watching less television, and the list goes on. But make sure the plan fits you. Clear mind is the goal!

To have a body that is fit, you need to be sure you are not sedentary. Some ideas are to exercise at least three times a week for twenty minutes each time. Just make sure you clear this with your medical doctor first.

Some of you may be able to exercise more if your health is good. Walking is great. Lifting weights is fine. There's also the part about eating fruits and vegetables and eliminating all caffeine and processed and fast foods. Stretching is beneficial here as well. Again, so many options, just make it your plan and stick to it. Fit body is the desired goal!

Finally, having a spirit that is well is so important. Remember that youth are at different developmental stages than adults. Therefore, we must approach them on their level or stage of development—no condescension, no judgment, display love and peace, read scripture or positive writings, pray, sing psalms, listen intently, and practice patience. Again, whatever you need to do so you can be healthy and engage youth, you need to do it and stick with it so you can reap the rewards that will come through a healthy connection. Well spirit is key!

78

# MIND CLEAR.

# BODY FIT.

# SPIRIT WELL.

# REFERENCES

Berk, L. "Development Through the Lifespan" 6th edition. Pearson: 2014.

Egan, G. "The Skilled Helper." *A Systematic Approach to Effective Helping* 3. (Belmont, CA: Brooks/Cole, 1986).

Mandela, N. Quote used Dec 6, 2013 and retrieved from https://www.usatoday.com/story/news/nation-now/2013/12/05/nelson-mandela-quotes/3775255/.

Sapp, J. F. "Exploring the Relationship Between Spiritual Well-Being, Religious Distress, and Depression Among College Students." (Northcentral University, 2011).

# ABOUT THE AUTHOR

Dr. James F. Sapp is a Licensed Professional Counselor/MHSP and a National Board-Certified Counselor who holds two doctoral degrees (PsyD and PhD). He has three decades of experience in working with youth and their families, from home-based services, to outpatient mental health, and inpatient psychiatric care. He has experience conducting international counseling. Since 2006, he has been teaching in higher education. Currently, he is an Associate Professor and Department Program Director of a Counseling and Psychology program. He is also a foster parent and continues to serve those in need of connecting with others.